HOW MY MIND HAS CHANGED

How My Mind Has Changed

Edited by

James M. Wall and David Heim

WILLIAM B. EERDMANS PUBLISHING COMPANY
GRAND RAPIDS, MICHIGAN

All the chapters in this book originally appeared as articles in
The Christian Century. Reprinted by permission.

Library of Congress Cataloging-in-Publication Data

How my mind has changed / edited by James M. Wall and David Heim.
p.   cm.
Reprints of essays originally published in Christian Century, 1990.
ISBN 0-8028-0533-7
1. Theology — 20th century. 2. Theologians. I. Wall, James M.
BR85.H588   1991
230 — dc20   91-9777
CIP

Contents

v

Contents

James M. Wall and David Heim

Introduction

In every decade for the past 50 years, *The Christian Century* has charted currents of religious life and thought by asking prominent figures to reflect on "how my mind has changed." When the series was first conceived at the end of the 1930s, the editors had witnessed a Great Depression, a New Deal, the rise of fascism in Europe and the emergence of neo-orthodox theology on both sides of the Atlantic. It seemed time for Protestant thinkers to do some stock-taking.

Not every ten-year span presents social and political changes that demand theological adjustment or response. For that matter, external events may be only tangentially related to the most significant kinds of theological reflection. Nevertheless, the question of how personal convictions have been formed, opinions reversed and projects begun remains a stimulating one for editors, authors and readers. Theology is disciplined study, but it is not disembodied. Behind theologians' work are journeys of faith and understanding. These essays reveal some steps of those journeys and record how individual biographies have intersected with social and intellectual history.

We invited the essayists to consider how social and political events captured their attention. We were equally curious about shifts in emphasis prompted by scholarly investigation and immediate experience. Above all, we wanted them to reflect on what topics most engage them now and on how those topics have taken shape.

The collection is clearly diverse. If ranged around one table, these voices would create a din of controversy or perhaps provoke some stunned silence. One imagines, at best, a wide-ranging, assumption-probing conversation — something William Placher nicely imagines in his retrospective essay. Such a conversation would itself be an achievement. One is easily tempted in these days of theological diversity to cut off the discussion, to resign oneself to incommunicability (perhaps with an appeal to pluralism) and to restrict oneself to more congenial conversation partners. In this collection we have tried to resist that temptation — tried to locate authors with lively stories and important claims that would open our conversation to the realities of God's world and the variousness of God's manifestation.

Even this much diversity is only a slice. It is, for one thing, focused on the U.S. scene. To extend our reach further in this case seemed to spread the conversation too thin. It is appropriate, however, that the exceptions are a priest from Central America, the site of much Christian witness and concern in the 1980s, and a theologian from a reunited Germany, where events of 1989 and 1990 outpaced any of our expectations of change.

The editors are grateful to the essayists for responding to our invitation to reflection. We also wish to thank the staff of the *Century* for helping shape the series, which appeared in the pages of the *Century* during 1990 and 1991. Special thanks to Dean Peerman, Mark Halton, Victoria A. Rebeck and Gretchen Ziegenhals for their editorial work; to Martin Marty for advice and encouragement; and to Patricia Olson, Dale Hasenick and Laura J. MacLean for attention to many details.

Stanley Hauerwas

The Testament of Friends

A team of evangelical Christians invaded Shipshewana, Indiana, to bring the lost of Shipshewana to Christ. In front of Yoder's drygoods store one of these earnest souls confronted a Mennonite farmer with the challenge, "Brother, are you saved?" The farmer was stunned by the question. All his years of attending the Peach Bloom Mennonite congregation had not prepared him for such a question — particularly in front of Yoder's.

Wanting not to offend, as well as believing that the person posing the question was of good will, he seriously considered how he might answer. After a long pause, the farmer asked his questioner for a pencil and paper and proceeded to list the names of ten people he believed knew him well. Most, he explained, were his friends but some were less than that and might even be enemies. He suggested that the evangelist ask these people whether they thought him saved since he certainly would not presume to answer such a question on his own behalf.

This story is one of my favorites, for it represents the way I have increasingly come to think of "my" work. Those who

Stanley Hauerwas is professor of theological ethics at the Divinity School at Duke University, Durham, North Carolina.

want to know "how my mind has changed" should ask my friends and enemies. This is not a gesture of humility about my thought or writing, but rather denotes my increasing theological, epistemological and moral conviction that theology in service to the church cannot come only from an individual mind. Anything worthwhile I have done is what my friends have done through me. Through my writing I discover previously unknown friends. They come forward, however, claiming me and in the process teach me how to understand what I have said, written or thought in a way that I had neither the courage nor imagination to think on my own.

So I am genuinely unsure how my mind has changed over the 22 years I have been teaching and writing. I am sure I am thinking about things now that had not even occurred to me 20 years ago. Old friends like David Burrell, Jim Burtchaell, Robert Wilken, Jim McClendon and Alasdair MacIntyre made me think about Aristotle, Aquinas and Wittgenstein in ways I had not anticipated. Even more important, they, along with many others, forced me to learn to pray — though in that I remain very much the novice. New friends, often graduate students, make me attend to the thought of Michel Foucault, Jacques Derrida and Gilles Deleuze. I believe that their ideas ought to make a difference not only about *what* I think but about *how* I think, though I must confess I am not sure I understand them well enough to know what difference they should make.

While learning new approaches, I am still exploring how Christian convictions require moral display for understanding what we might mean to claim them as true. I also continue to believe that the virtues can help display those convictions, though I now try to avoid talking so abstractly about "the virtues" and focus more on concrete virtues such as patience and hope. I continue to be surprised by how this agenda has led me to appreciate the integrity of Christian discourse — that is, that Christian beliefs do not need translation but should be demonstrated through Christian practices, not the least of which is friendship of and in a concrete community. The radical social and political implications of such practices continue to challenge me, as I am sure Christians must rethink their concordat with institutions and regimes formed by liberal presuppositions.

To call my concerns "an agenda" may be too grand. I certainly do not have "a systematic position." I remember after I published my first collection of essays, *Vision and Virtue* (1974), Richard Bondi, one of my first graduate students, asked me whether I was going to spend the rest of my life defending the position I had developed in that book. I said I sure would if I could just remember what the position was. Unfortunately, I am unable to remember "my position" or the arguments I use to support it. Without friends to remember my claims I am at a complete loss. But I discover that in their remembering, which is often expressed in disagreements, there is often more than I knew. I continue to be graced with graduate students who understand me better than I understand myself and can show me where I have got it wrong.

Even though I have trouble remembering my position, I do know what I care about. Over the past 20 or so years I have discovered that others expect me to be a theologian in and for the church of Jesus Christ. It is at once a wonderful gift and a frightening realization, since only God knows how one can be faithful to that most ambiguous of vocations. But at least I do not have the burden of being "a thinker" — that is, someone who, philosopher-like, develops strong opinions that bear the stamp of individual genius. My task is rather to take what friends — living and dead, some Christian and some not — have given me to help the church be faithful to the wonderful adventure we call Kingdom. Theology, of course, is one of the lesser services the church provides, but I do care about, and thus find great joy in, studying and developing it. That is why I do not have to remember "my position"; it is the activity of theology I care about.

My claim to be a theologian is not unlike my claim to be a pacifist. I often refer to myself as the latter though I very much dislike the term "pacifist" — to name "pacifism" as its own field of interest seems to imply that it is intelligible apart from the cross and resurrection of Jesus. Yet I think it important to claim the position even at the risk of being misunderstood. To make the claim not only begins the argument but, more important, creates expectations in others that should help me live nonviolently. I have no faith in my ability to live that way because I know I am filled with violence. However, I hope by creating expectations in others that they will come to love me well enough to help me live according to the way of life I believe to be true. In like manner I find that others often use what I think to force me to be not just a thinker but a theologian.

Yet even the claim that I am a theologian, that I have been called to serve the church through the activity of theology, may be self-deceptive. The assertion challenges me to point out the church that has actually commissioned me, the church that I actually serve. It questions whether the church I write about actually exists. It taunts me that I am not a church theologian but just another academic theologian who continues to draw off the residual resources of Constantinian Christianity to fantasize about a church that does not and probably cannot or should not exist, given the political and economic realities of our time.

That challenge hurts because I know there is truth in it. The emphasis I have put on the faithful church as integral for demonstrating the truthfulness of Christian convictions makes the challenge all the more powerful. I cannot escape by distinguishing between visible or invisible church, by appealing to ideals always yet to be realized, or by suggesting that the theologian's task is to describe what the church ought to be, not what it is. My church must exist as surely as the Jews have to be God's promised people. That, of course, is why I cannot do without friends who live their convictions more faithfully than I write. At best I try to be a witness to their lives.

"Friends" do not constitute "church." Yet many of my friends are churched. Among them are liberal and conservative

Roman Catholics, some Southern Baptists, some evangelicals, some Presbyterians, some Mennonites, some Calvinists, some Episcopalians, some Lutherans (not many), some from the Church of the Servant King (Gardenia, California), some liberal Protestants, some feminists and some liberationists. Even some Methodists tell me that though they disagree with certain details, generally they find my ideas helpful. But how can that be? Paul may have thought he should be all things to all people, but that is probably not good advice for theologians. Perhaps I am useful to such diverse communities because the disputes of the past are simply not all that relevant to the challenge to remain church today.

Another explanation for the breadth of my range of friends is that I am a Texas Methodist who went to Yale, came under the influence of Barth and Wittgenstein, taught two years for the Lutherans at Augustana College (Rock Island, Illinois), and 14 for the Catholics at Notre Dame, and have ended up with the Methodists at Duke. It is a wonderful gift to have been part of so many different communities, but it often makes me wonder who I am. I remember how this became clear to me at a Notre Dame departmental retreat where we were discussing, one more time, what it meant to be a theology department in a Catholic school. The Missouri-Synod Lutheran said what it meant to be part of such a department as a person of his tradition, as did the Dutch Calvinist, the Jesuit and the Mennonite. I sat in uncharacteristic silence trying to figure out what it meant for me to be there as a Methodist. Suddenly I thought, "Hell, I'm not a Methodist. I went to Yale!"

This story expresses the melancholy truth that for most of us theologians, where we went to graduate school informs our self-understanding more than our denominational identification does. As a result, we think of ourselves as Bultmannians, Barthians, process theologians, feminists or liberationists rather than as Methodists, Presbyterians, Anglicans or, perhaps, even Christians. That I went to Yale in the mid-'60s is, I suspect, the reason I am subject to so many influences from so many different ecclesial communities, and so useful to such a wide range of groups. For at Yale I was taught to engage in theology as a traditioned-determined practice that is not determined by any one tradition — other than Yale's. It is no wonder I care so deeply for the church: it is the only protection I have against Yale.

I suppose my Yale breeding is one reason why I find the charges that I am a "fideistic, sectarian tribalist" so puzzling. Admittedly, I have been and continue to be strongly influenced by John Howard Yoder. I like to think of myself as a Mennonite camp follower — an odd image, but I think the Mennonites need camp followers as otherwise they might forget they are an army in one hell of a fight. But to admit that I have been influenced by Yoder does not make me sectarian, for as Yoder eloquently argues in *The Priestly Kingdom,* he is not a Mennonite theologian but a theologian of the church catholic. Yoder taught me that the mainstream's celebration of pluralism is the way the mainstream maintains its assumption of its superiority. Thus "we" understand, and perhaps appreciate, the "sects" better than they can appreciate themselves. The one with the most inclusive typology wins the game.

That I was trained at Yale does not sufficiently account for the fact I seem to belong nowhere, for as I noted, I went to Yale as a Texas Methodist. I was and remain more Texan than Methodist, though both have strongly shaped my identity. Because I was raised Texan — which is like being southern, only better — I knew I was never free to be "modern" and "self-creating." I would always be, for better or worse, Texan. It was my first lesson in particularity; as some would put it, being Texan made me realize early that the foundationalist epistemologies of the Enlightenment had to be wrong. I am unsure, however, that I want to be an antifoundationalist since that would make me too dependent on the way foundationalists tell the story. I prefer simply to have a Texan epistemology.

I also went to Yale as a Methodist. Admittedly, I was not a very good one, but it was unclear then and is unclear now what it means to be a good one. Methodism, after all, is a movement that by accident became a church. Yet at least on some tellings of our story we are a theologically interesting accident; that is, we are a catholic church with a free-church polity.

So by describing myself as a high-church Mennonite I am saying I am a Methodist. Methodist identity makes sense only as it entails a commitment to discovering the unity of God's church through our different histories.

If my work has some use in different ecclesial traditions, I suspect it is partly because as a Methodist I am not theologically subtle. I am impressed that churches baptize, preach, serve the eucharist, call some to serve the church and send some to serve in the world. If my work has any center it has been to help Christians across God's church discover the moral significance of these extraordinary yet everyday practices.

That may seem odd for one who is often described as a radical — a description I certainly prefer to liberal or conservative. Yet I continue to believe that nothing is more radical than the existence of a people who worship the God we know by the names Father, Son and Holy Spirit. All that I have said about virtue, narrative or the political significance of the church has been an attempt to help us reclaim what is already there. I do not believe that God has abandoned the church or that the church is so compromised that it is incapable of witness. I am confident that God can be trusted to make the church — that is where Jesus is worshiped—serve the Kingdom.

I have gone through some changes, however; not the least concerning my emphasis on the centrality of the church. I began seeking to recover the importance of virtue and the virtues and ended up with the church. In a new introduction to *Character and the Christian Life* I note that I had in this book mistakenly tried to generate an account of agency from an analysis of action qua action, thus failing to see, as MacIntyre has taught us, that action can be analyzed only in a context. In spite of my attempt to provide an alternative to Kantian-inspired accounts of morality, I continued to support too uncritically the isolated "I." In that book I tried to isolate Aristotle's account of virtue from his account of happiness and friendship. As a result, moreover, that book could not but appear apolitical.

That is why I cannot write an account of how "I" am making up my mind: I have increasingly come to distrust the moral psychology that maintains the existence of such an "I." The "self" of self-agency, assumed in my early work, still owed too much to the self abstracted from any narrative—something Derrida and Foucault have rightly questioned. I have been very lucky to live at a time of such rich intellectual developments. As a result I now think I understand much better how a narrative is necessary for character — or to put it theologically, why sin and forgiveness are necessary for us to be "selves" — and as an alternative to Descartes and Kant as well as their geneological critics.

I am quite sure that the way Christians should live can be displayed without Aristotle, and perhaps even without, as Yoder never ceases to remind me, the virtues. Moreover, the Christian conviction that our "happiness" is the gift of a God who determines all existence through the cross of Christ requires a radically transformed understanding of happiness, the virtues and friendship. I cannot let these questions go, for I remain convinced that any truthful account of Christian convictions requires a display of the sanctified life.

At the same time that I have been writing about happiness I have also been writing a book on the suffering and death of children, *Naming the Silences: God, Medicine and the Problem of Suffering.* I am increasingly convinced that Christians are capable of joy because their hopes make them vulnerable to suffering. Though this book is meant to be pastoral, it also explores the epistemological and social presumptions that produced the idea of *the* problem of evil. I aim to provide a different perspective on medicine as well as suggest a different approach to medical ethics. In the name of freeing us from suffering, modern medicine and its correlative ethical expressions have become our fate — which we now impose on our children by not understanding their suffering and death through a more determinative narrative.

I am happier about this book than anything I have done for some time. It is short and I hope accessible to people who have not had the disadvantage of a theological education. In that respect I am trying to resist the professionalization of theology, which I consider a Babylonian captivity of theology by the Enlightenment university. If I had the talent I would even like to write a "popular" book. But I know I do not have the talent for such an undertaking. I also continue to put together books that combine some fairly difficult philosophical discussions with essays that I hope are entertaining. I do so not because I am trying to use more popular essays to entice some to read the more "serious" essays — indeed, I think that the more popular essays are the more serious — but because, I am convinced, as a friend has put it, that "arguments, including moral arguments, cannot be separated from the descriptions that not merely accompany them, but make them possible."

That I understand theology to be a descriptive task may be one of the reasons so many misunderstand or resist my work. I am not suggesting that if people understood me better they would agree with me; I suspect the opposite is the case. But I think some try to force me into a predetermined category — i.e., liberal or conservative, in theology or politics — when in fact I am trying to challenge the very presuppositions that have created those categories. For example, I prefer to ignore the oft-made charge that I am a "sectarian" — though I could not resist responding to that notion in *Christian Existence Today*, since I am challenging the epistemologies and social theories that generate the unhappy normative use of that typology.

Perhaps the most difficult descriptive issue I have addressed is the theological and moral status of war. I am disappointed that no one has significantly challenged the case I made for the moral significance of war in *Against the Nations* — except for Paul Ramsey in his wonderful book *Speak Up for*

Just War or Pacifism. Ramsey and I originally planned to write essays of equal length criticizing the Methodist bishops' pastoral letter, "In Defense of Creation." But by the time Ramsey finished his extraordinary critique it was clear that all I needed to do was write an epilogue. Though Ramsey and I disagreed, I hope our exchange illumines the descriptive power of Christian convictions. Nothing has honored me more than Paul Ramsey's claiming me as friend.

I have said little about how changes in our society, the church and my own life have forced me to think about things differently or to think about matters I had not imagined when I began. None of us can be or should be immune from such influence, but with this essay I wanted at least to gesture toward what I learned through friends. Friends have taught me how wonderful and frightening it is to be called to serve in God's kingdom.

Carter Heyward

The Power of God-with-Us

1 980: The dawn of *Nicaragua libre* and the impending U.S. presidency of Reagan, its ardent foe. A time in which the pernicious AIDS virus was moving among us, and we were unaware. Three years before the invasion of Grenada and six before the falls of Marcos and Duvalier. Before the emergence of *glasnost* and of Gorbachev. Just before the beginning of death-dealing cutbacks in already-small measures of care for people of color, women, children, others marginalized and animals, plants and minerals of many sorts in the U.S. The outset of a high-tech boom that would threaten further to diminish our senses of ourselves as co-subjects in the sensual work and play of creation. In this context, I was studying black, feminist and Latin American liberation theologies and was becoming convinced that a justice-making church could make a difference in the world.

Winding up a dissertation on a "theology of mutual relation" would, ironically, provide my fare into the security of a profession not well known for the mutuality of its practices or

---

Carter Heyward, professor of theology at the Episcopal Divinity School in Cambridge, Massachusetts, is a lesbian feminist theologian of liberation.

its theories. But, at age 35, I would be officially out of school for the first time in 30 years, and I leaped into the decade with a blessing in my pocket worth more than the Ph.D. — unbounded enthusiasm for the theological vocation. Amid ups and downs, delights and sufferings, deaths and births, burnout and rekindling, I have been carried by the past decade more fully into an appreciation of honest theological work. I have been learning to recognize it, at its root, as a spiritual passion that we need in the world and that the world needs in us.

Let me back up a little. Though I was a graduate student, full- or part-time, for over a decade, my studies had not done much to deliver me from life. Working at Union Seminary in New York and in the city itself, in parishes, hospitals and shelters, I was learning as much about human life as about its divine source and resource.

I remember sitting under a tree in the summer of 1980 with United Methodist minister Michael Collins (who later would die of AIDS) and several other members of the minuscule gay-lesbian caucus of the Theologies in the Americas "Detroit II" conference. We spoke of how grateful we were to be learning with our theological "elders" that the sacred spirit of life can be experienced as the power moving us in the making of justice with compassion and of peace with justice.

I was sure that, sooner or later, the church would get it. Surely the liberal christian communities would come to see the rightness of the theologies of liberation being generated globally by christians and others struggling for bread and dignity.* The basis of my optimism was, I believe, no facile "liberalism." In the company of discerning teachers and learners, my education was being shaped out of certain assumptions that had as much to do with living life as with thinking about it: that we are "in relation"

---

*Using the lowercase "c" with reference to "christianity" is a spiritual discipline for me as a member of a religious tradition so arrogant and abusive in its exercise of *power over* women, lesbians and gays, indigenous people, Jews, Muslims and members of nonchristian religions and cultures.

whatever we may think of that fact, that the most basic human unit is not therefore "the self" but rather "the relation"; and that this intrinsic mutuality demands — and should be the foundation of — our ethics, politics, pastoral care and theologies.

Drawing on the existential theology and social philosophy of Martin Buber, I wrote in my thesis that God is our "power in relation" and that justice, the actualization of love among us, is the making of right, or mutual, relation. Without realizing it I was trying to articulate a relational *ontology* as a companion piece to the profoundly *moral* motives and commitments of liberation theology.

My graduate studies had sparked my interest in human life as a relational matrix in which God is born. (The coming decade would stretch my imagination toward an intense interest in the connectedness of all life.) I felt a certain euphoria upon graduation. Happily donning a yellow button on my academic gown that read, "Better Gay than Grumpy," I stepped into the '80s and the ranks of professional theology as an active, indignant and optimistic teacher and priest with a ragged-edged commitment to justice for all oppressed people.

The past ten years have brought me to some new places — more exactly, I suppose, into new ways of standing in old commitments and values. It is not simply that "my mind" has changed. My mind — how I think theologically — would have to have been put on ice not to be changing in some degree of conformity with its relational matrix.

Maybe as it grays, every theological generation loses some of its youthful idealism. But if, in changing (as we must to stay well), we do not hold stubbornly to the roots of this idealism, we will be sucked into a funnel through which our theological vision will narrow and, in time, become rigid and false. I am disappointed in my generational peers who look back upon "the '60s" with patronizing scorn, as if we ought to be a little embarrassed for having dreamed those dreams. I am learning that I do not trust those whose dreams become less daring with time.

I am not as busy as I was ten or 20 years ago. There's still much to do and I may be better able to do some of it, but I am doing less. I am not as optimistic as I was that organized religion will make much headway in creating a more just and compassionate world. I now understand better the conservative character and structure of the church, having been working within it (or at its edges) as a priest for about 16 years. I am less idealistic. I do not expect that many who hold authority in the church or other dominant institutions of our lives will be converted, en masse or as individuals, to the serious work of justice-making with compassion and good humor as their top priority. But I'm not cynical. My faith in the power of God-with-us — our creative, liberating power with one another — is secure, and my hope for the world is being radicalized. My companions in living, working and visioning; the claims of justice; and the urgings of the spirit are pushing me closer to the roots of the idealism and enthusiasm I embraced ten years ago. I am beginning to imagine the implications of the connectedness of all life, my own and that of other humans and creatures. I see more completely the importance of living in such a way as to celebrate the struggle for mutuality (the actual dynamic of justice-making) not only as an ethical ideal but as the very essence of who we are in the world — the basis of our survival. I am learning that, in this sense, our we-ness literally creates my I-ness and that this is a very great good. It is the foundation of what it means to be human, what it means to be "in the image of God."

My learning has been partially the result of a *via negativa*, recognizing not only the absence of mutuality and justice but an active opposition to it in the doctrines of selfishness and domination incarnate in Reagan-Bush. I am at least as indignant today as ever and no less hesitant to say so. I am angry that a culture of alienation and despair, of greed and violence, is being constructed for profit on the bodies of the poor, the elderly, the young, women, blacks, browns, gays, lesbians and other people in the U.S., and is being masked as "kindliness" and "gentle-

14

ness" by those who have learned to believe their own lies. Beverly Wildung Harrison, my beloved friend and companion through the past decade, reminds me of "the power of anger in the work of love."

If good humor is, at heart, a sense of perspective, I think I am maintaining it by *enjoying* being alive in the world. I delight in my friends, my students, my niece and nephew, movies and music, my animal companions, and our little bit of land and home on the Maine coast. I love walking and dancing and singing and laughing.

Still, I suspect that those who do not care for pushy broads, feminist priests, happy dykes and faggots, and irreverent references to the god of heterosexist, racist patriarchy, are likely to find me every bit as ornery as before. Recent years have dipped me into the wisdom of sages like feminist theorist Judith McDaniel who warn that trying to be "nice" on terms set by those who hold the power in place is to "sell ourselves short."

Specifically, then, what am I learning? *I am learning that, without some serenity, I could not continue in the struggle for justice.* Like that of many U.S. citizens visiting in Nicaragua during the '80s, my time there, in 1983 and 1984, was an unexpected blessing. I did not go seeking a gift. I went to be educated and to show solidarity with those struggling against the contras. In fact, my traveling companions and I were given a glimpse into the life of a people fighting enormous odds for the chance to live together in a just and peaceful society. Scores of Nicaraguan christians and others met us with what seemed unflappable confidence in themselves and in their spiritual or moral vocation to struggle for justice.

Not until I had been back in the U.S. for several months did it dawn on me that I had experienced a profound sense of serenity in these people and, through them, had glimpsed my own confidence and inner strength, elusive through much of my life as a white christian in the U.S.

I have wondered why so many white people have learned in Nicaragua what we well might have learned here at home —

15

in active, ongoing solidarity with, for example, black sisters and brothers or Native Americans. Has it been easier to go to a faraway land to see what has been happening right before our eyes? Easier because it felt safer, less intimate, or because we did not know how significantly our lives would be touched until it was too late to stop the transformation?

Nicaragua shook my foundations. As the experience grew in me, I found my commitments stronger than ever and, at the same time, I knew that I could not, in the words of womanist ethicist Katie Cannon, "keep on keepin' on." I was outraged about U.S. imperialism; hurt and angry about how women and gay and lesbian people are treated everywhere, especially in the church; horrified by the blatantly racist practices of the Reagan administration; immensely saddened by the death of my father; frightened by a breast cancer scare; working too hard in a seminary that drains its feminist professors to meet the demands of increasing numbers of women students; and just plain tired.

It took me several years to see that, in the early '80s, my faith was in serious crisis. As I left for Nicaragua, I was burning out. Had I ever, really, believed in resurrection? Had it ever occurred to me, deep in my soul, that it is a relational movement, the revolutionary carrying-on of a spirit of love and justice that does not and will not die? Had I ever truly believed that the Spirit needs us to do her work in the world, to move as slowly as we must in order to build this world together as a common home? Had I seen fully that we are never called to come forth alone but always to answer the Spirit's call *with* one another, drawing for strength and wisdom from what womanist theologian Delores Williams calls our "lines of continuity"?

This trust in the foundations of one's life has roots in the experience of right, mutual relationship. Thus at the core of our faith we know that, in the beginning and in the end, we are not alone. In our living and in our dying, we are not separate from one another. Reminiscent of Jesus, Martin Luther King, Jr., and others who have seen this, Archbishop Oscar Romero prophetically voiced this confidence when he promised, "If they kill me,

I will rise again in the Salvadorean people. . . . My hope is that my blood will be like a seed of liberty."

In the strength of such faith, an inner peace can begin to form. Perhaps this incipient confidence enabled me in 1985 to speak to a friend, a former student, about my "drinking problem" and to hear his response: "It troubles me that someone who teaches and writes so much about mutuality is so resistant to seeing that you need help with this. You can't stop drinking alone. Why don't you take your own theology seriously?" A theophany, this encounter.

The next morning, with another friend, I attended my first meeting with other alcoholics and began recovering, one day at a time. In the spirit of the Nicaragua pilgrimage, this process is opening me to the real presence of others and myself to them. It is opening us to the power released among us in a vulnerability that, because it is authentic, common and shared, is sacred.

I don't believe any more now than before that we must participate in organized religion to be involved in the work of justice. But I know today that all of us need a shared sense of a spiritual or moral basis upon which to build our lives and commitments.

I am learning the critical necessity of approaching our theological work the same way we do any authentic spirituality: through the particularities of our lives-in-relation. A hermeneutic of particularity involves studying ways in which our differences contribute to how we experience and think about human and divine life.

In a racist society, a black god/ess is not at all the same as a white god/ess. In a hetero/sexist situation, a goddess is different from a god. In a sex-negative culture, an erotically empowering spirit is utterly distinct from an asexual and erotophobic god who needs no friends.

Through the work primarily of feminist christians, I have been led to Sophia/Wisdom, to "Christa/community," to Hagar the slave woman, to Jephthah's daughter and those who fight

17

back on her behalf: images that are redemptive *because* they are dark, images of black or marginalized women, vilified, trivialized, rejected, silenced — and resisting their oppression and that of their sisters. As our historical imaginations unfold, we may begin to recognize in these images a call to struggle against injustice and to celebrate our woman-lives.

A goddess whose tender, outraged presence heals and strengthens abused women is entirely different from the God in whose name troubled fathers and priests sometimes rape girls and boys. I have been taught this less by my feminist professional colleagues than by the students who have attended my classes on passes from hospitals or after therapy sessions, in which they are being treated for wounds inflicted by men (and sometimes women) who abused them as children or as adults. Their stories often suggest the appalling extent to which the church tends not simply to ignore sexual, physical, emotional and spiritual violence against women and children as a major crisis, but actually to provide theological justification for this violence in its teachings about male headship, women's subordination, and the sinful character of sexuality. The sex-as-sin obsession which characterizes christianity has produced a repressive, guilt-inducing sexual ethic which, in turn, generates a pornographic culture of eruptive sexual violence.

I am learning that I cannot teach christian theology constructively unless I am aware that, historically, the church has done much to damage women, Jews, people of color and the whole inhabited earth; and unless, as a christian, I am learning how our doctrine, discipline and worship continue to reflect and contribute to this abuse of power.

I also have become clearer during this violent decade that it matters a great deal what god-images we use in our worship. I am becoming increasingly resistant to participating in, much less leading, liturgy from which dark, erotically empowering, woman-loving images of God are absent or concealed. The election and consecration of Barbara Harris as an Episcopal bishop signaled hope for many of us. This was not because either the Episcopal Church or one powerful, capable woman, black and beautiful and prophetic, will move mountains. It was rather because the choosing of such a bishop — by the-Republican-Party-at-prayer-church of George Bush and Sandra Day O'Connor — conveyed the kind of lovely, unexpected contradiction that christians love to call "paradox." Bishop Harris is a living, breathing reminder that just about anything can happen when two or three are gathered in the spirit of justice.

During these ten years, my understanding of God has been, to quote radical feminist Mary Daly, "gyn/ecologized." I believe that God is indeed our power in mutual relation. I see more vividly than before that our redemption requires that this power come to us, and through us, in healing and liberation, advocacy and friendship, love and sisterliness, in the most badly broken and frightening places of our life together and as individuals. In a racist, heterosexist, class-injured world, God is likely to meet us often in images associated with children, poor women, black, brown, yellow and red women, lesbian women, battered women, bleeding women and women learning to fight back. Dark images. Like Mary's poor little boy, God is seldom welcome in reputable places. The story is not a nice one. Good theology is not respectable.

I am learning that, as a process of liberation from either injustice or despair, healing is a process of finding — if need be, creating — redemption in suffering. The AIDS crisis has been teaching me this, as did my father's nine-year bout with cancer, which resulted in his death in 1984. More recently, the sickness and death of a young friend, and a devastating relational rupture that left me badly hurt and in need of healing, have required me to struggle with the meaning of suffering.

As we move into the '90s with an economic structure that is killing poor people, a "war against drugs" that is a racist war against the urban poor, an unapologetic "post-feminist" contempt for women and girls and a mounting ecological crisis, we will need as much as ever to be able to create liberation in the midst of suffering.

I have never believed in "redemptive suffering" as a means of justifying either pain or God. I still do not. There is no theological excuse for the pain inflicted upon human and other creatures by human beings. There is no justification, no spiritual reason, why forces of nature such as hurricanes and viruses hurt us or why some of us get hit by cars or lost when planes crash. The death of my life-loving father was not good, nor was death of my friend Dianna, nor the agony of her spouse and family. From a theological perspective, whether pastoral or ethical, suffering is not good for us.

Although the sacred Spirit in no way "wills" or sets us up for suffering, all living creatures do suffer. In these last years, scarred by AIDS, by the dominant culture of greed and violence, and by personal loss and pain, I have come to see more distinctly the vital link between the healing process (traditionally the prerogative of religious and medical traditions) and the work of liberation (assumed to be the business of revolutionary movements for justice).

The link is in the commitment of those who suffer and of those in solidarity with them to make no peace with whatever injustice or abuse is causing or contributing to their suffering, *and* in their commitment to celebrate the goodness and power in our relationships with one another — especially, in these moments, with those who suffer. To struggle against the conditions that make for or exacerbate suffering, and to do so with compassion — "suffering with" one another — is how we find redemption in suffering. To realize the sacred power in our relationships with one another, and to contend against the forces that threaten to damage and destroy us, bears luminous witness to the goodness and power of God. In the midst of suffering, we weave our redemption out of solidarity and compassion, struggle and hope. In this way, we participate in the redemption of God.

Richard J. Mouw

Humility, Hope and the Divine Slowness

John Reeve, the 17th-century leader of the British sect known as the Muggletonians, strongly opposed the idea of an earthly millennial kingdom. He was convinced that Jesus had no interest in returning to earth to establish a political administration. After all, he asked, didn't Jesus suffer during his last stay on earth? Why would he want to come back as a politician and suffer again? I must confess that I am tempted, as I think back over this past decade as an evangelical social ethicist, to add my own spin to Reeve's argument. Even if Jesus didn't suffer enough during his first earthly tour of duty, isn't it likely that he has had his fill of "Christian politics" by now? Hasn't his capacity at least for political suffering finally reached its limit?

Ten years ago I was devoting much attention to the New Christian Right. At the beginning of the 1980s, "born-again politics" was being heralded as a major new force in North America. It is clear today, however, that the New Christian Right lacked the vision and leadership to live up to its promise — or

---

Richard J. Mouw is provost of Fuller Theological Seminary in Pasadena, California.

even to justify the fears of its opponents. While many New Rightists remain active in the abortion controversy, the enthusiasm for a more comprehensive political program has dissipated. The Moral Majority no longer exists, and several prominent New Right preachers have experienced public humiliation.

I did not altogether oppose born-again politics when it appeared on the scene. I spent my early years as an ethicist trying to convince my evangelical kinfolk that the gospel does indeed have clear political implications. The New Christian Right signaled a change of agenda: the arguments with Bible-believing Christians about whether the gospel is in fact political gave way to questions about the actual content of Christian politics. This struck me as an important advance.

And it was. Evangelicals are more aware these days of the political dimensions of the gospel than they were 20 years ago. But it is also clear that they have much theological homework to do on social, political and economic questions.

A staff member of a mainline church told me after a speech I gave recently that, much to his surprise, he agreed with just about everything I said. "Tell me," he asked, "how does a person like you survive in the evangelical world?" One thing that helps, I replied, is that I really am an evangelical.

Labels can outlive their usefulness, and those of us who insist upon being called "evangelical" must be sensitive to changing alignments in the Christian world. But I still find it helpful to assume a label that points to the centrality of the evangel, the good news that Jesus Christ came into the world to save sinners.

To be sure, there is more to the gospel than a message about individual salvation. But there is not *less* to the gospel than that. I am encouraged by the increasing Christian awareness that proper discipleship requires us to take up the causes of peace, justice and righteousness. But no program of liberation is fully adequate that does not offer people the new life that comes from a personal acceptance of the claims of the gospel.

It is precisely this strong emphasis on the personal dimension, of course, that has made it so difficult for evangelicals to think clearly about structural issues. The categories necessary for a theological understanding of corporate life do not come easily for us. The situation is further complicated by the fact that the current of anti-intellectualism flowing through most pietism — and the North American conservative evangelical community is essentially a coalition of pietist movements — makes it difficult for evangelicals to work hard at mastering those categories.

Evangelical political embarrassments of this past decade are due in good part, I am convinced, to this kind of theological failure. New Right preachers were unable to cultivate a political perspective that could provide the nuances and staying power necessary for coping with complex political realities. Furthermore, their past patterns of cultural and ecclesiastical separatism have left them with few role models outside of their own groups. I for one would have been immensely pleased if, for example, Jerry Falwell and Pat Robertson had gone to the Roman Catholic bishops for some private tutoring on matters of public moral pedagogy.

When it comes to political discussion, evangelical Christianity very much needs to cultivate those "communities of memory" whose cultural importance was underscored by the authors of *Habits of the Heart*. The resources of a forgotten past must be mined for their present relevance. Some people are already attempting to do this. For example, evangelical colleges and seminaries are conducting promising discussions on a variety of traditions of ethical discourse, including Anabaptist, Reformed, Franciscan, Puritan, African-American and Wesleyan. These ethical explorations must be intensified, and more time must be spent probing some very basic questions.

As a teenager I read J. B. Phillips's *Your God Is Too Small*. Though I can't remember any of the book's contents, the title has served me well as a reference point for thinking about the doctrine of God. Throughout my adult life I have regularly asked myself what variation on Phillips's title best summarizes how I and my closest spiritual kinfolk are limiting the deity. In the 1960s I came to see that my understanding of God had been too interwoven with racism and nationalism. During the next decade I thought much about how my concept of the deity had been too North Atlantic. The 1980s have given me opportunity to think about how patriarchal assumptions have distorted the doctrine of God.

Obviously, we learn none of those theological lessons once and for all. They are subject to ongoing reflection. But if I had to choose the variation on Phillips's title that best captures my most recent exercises in corrective theology, it would be *your God is too fast.*

I have been thinking a lot about God's "pace" in recent years. The importance of this topic became strikingly clear to me over lunch during an ecumenical consultation a few years ago. The small group at my table consisted of evangelicals and Roman Catholics. Somehow the question of "creation science" came up. While none of the evangelicals present promoted the idea of a literal six-day creation, we all had close ties to people who held literalist interpretations. So we tried to explain the phenomenon to our Catholic friends, putting the best face that we could on the literal-creationist perspective.

The Catholics had a difficult time generating any sympathy for the position we were outlining. Finally one Catholic scholar threw her hands up in despair, exclaiming in an agitated voice, "Don't these people realize that God likes to do things *slowly?*"

Her rhetorical question brought the issues into sharp focus for me. What she took for granted is precisely what many of my evangelical kinfolk do *not* realize; they insist that God likes to work fast. They think the only proper way to honor God as the creator of all things is to assert that God created everything quickly. And what holds for the deity's "macro" dealings with the universe applies also to the "micro" issue of individual salvation; if a person has genuinely been "saved," she would have known when it happened — there is no mistaking the salvific activity of a God who is fond of doing things quickly and decisively.

I am convinced that one reason evangelicals have such difficulty taking questions of racial and economic justice seriously is that the problems in those areas seem so intractable. If God works quickly and decisively, then the fact that these problems haven't been solved yet must mean that God doesn't care very much about these particular areas of human concern.

The obvious defects of this way of viewing the processes of social change point to the need for a proper theological understanding of divine slowness. Both Catholic and Reformed thought provide resources for developing a deep appreciation for a more deliberate divine pace. In each case — exemplified by the Reformed fascination with the idea of providence and the Roman emphasis on the development of dogma — the notion of human history as an arena for the developmental unfolding of the divine purposes looms large.

The developmental understanding of God's attitude toward history does have important psychological and cultural corollaries. The *imitatio dei* seems to play a role here — we tend to adjust our human pace according to our sense of how fast God is moving. The Reformed community has a long history of resisting all-at-once, perfectionist schemes, both in its understanding of the individual spiritual pilgrimage and in its programs of political reform. And my Roman Catholic friends are fond of quoting the Ignatian reminder that "God uses crooked sticks to draw straight lines" — a sentiment that would sound very strange to many evangelical ears.

These less dramatic expectations seem quite appropriate to me these days, as do the theological themes that serve as their foundation. Not that I have sworn off everything associated with the theology of quickness and decisiveness. In his study of "immediatism" in antislavery movements, historian David Brion Davis distinguishes between a subjective immediatism, according to which people directly and forthrightly condemned the slavery system, and a more programmatic immediatism, which looked for quick and simple solutions to the problem.

On many issues I am a subjective immediatist. Apartheid, for example, is a phenomenon that seems to demand decisive moral clarity. It is the more programmatic variety of immediatism that makes me nervous. But I would not even condemn that without qualification. I celebrate the sudden conversions that many individuals have experienced, and those signs of God's active intervention in human affairs force me to accept the possibility of sudden conversions of social structures as well. But I don't expect them as simply a matter of course.

Nothing about this new appreciation for development and slowness means that I have become a neoconservative. To be sure, I have learned some important lessons from the neoconservative movement, which has become an important voice in Christian dialogue about public policy during this past decade. At the very least, neoconservatism has helped me to understand more clearly the uneasiness that I have long felt toward the political and economic remedies that liberationist and radical Christian thinkers sometimes advocate. In that respect the neoconservative movement has introduced some balance into the intellectual dialogue.

One important lesson that we all should have learned from the neoconservatives by now is that the intentions behind many of our efforts on behalf of the poor and the oppressed do not always match the results. Indeed, immediatist-interventionist solutions often make matters worse in the long run. Furthermore, the fact that a specific policy or system does not intentionally aim at bettering the lot of the oppressed does not mean that it will not in fact eventually produce beneficial effects for them; poverty-stricken people are often served better by schemes that emphasize the production of wealth than they are by redistributionist programs. Those things seem to me to be important for Christians to admit.

But we must also acknowledge that not all immediatist-interventionist solutions fail to deliver what they promise. And not all that encourages the production of wealth benefits the poor in the long run. Thus I am also nervous about neoconservatism.

I have developed a cautious attitude toward programmatic solutions offered in the name of the gospel. But I do not face the next decade without reference points for evaluating programmatic proposals. I am convinced, for example, that the God of the Bible does want us to commit ourselves to the cause of the poor and the oppressed. A willingness to focus on this cause in a very sustained and serious manner is itself an important reference point in formulating public policy. This doesn't eliminate the need for continued discussion about who among the wretched of the earth most need our direct ministry of compassion and empowerment. A serious dialogue about that topic can be very healthy, especially when accompanied by the firm conviction that the issues are so important that informed risk-taking is an urgent necessity.

Another subject I've confronted is pluralism. I am more ecumenical at the end of this decade than I was at the beginning in that I have a deeper appreciation for the ways in which God's gracious dealings with the Christian community make positive use of a variety of theological, denominational and liturgical schemes. I have become more pluralistic not merely in accepting plurality as a fact of life, but in considering some kinds of diversity to be very healthy for Christians.

One place in which I have been exploring the relationship between pluralism and ecumenism is in the book-length manuscript on public pluralism that I have been writing with a philosophy colleague, Sander Griffioen of the Free University of Amsterdam. This research project has occupied much of my scholarly attention for the past ten years.

Other events have reinforced this interest. Most important has been my move in 1985 from Calvin College, a midwestern school known for its strong Dutch Calvinist identity, to a west coast evangelical seminary characterized by a fascinating mix of denominational and cross-cultural diversity. I have discovered Fuller Seminary to be an exciting experiment in what David Hubbard describes as "evangelical ecumenism."

Also during the past decade I have as a board member and as an active participant in various consultations worked with the Institute for Ecumenical and Cultural Research in Collegeville, Minnesota. This experience of wrestling with ecumenical issues has profoundly influenced my understanding of the proper contours of theological pluralism.

The institute's unique "first-person approach" to ecumenical dialogue has allowed me to be ecumenical without compromising my sense of evangelical integrity. And it has also provided me with a circle of Roman Catholic, Orthodox and mainline Protestant mentor-friends — Margaret O'Gara, Tom Stransky, Tony Ugolnik, Roberta Bondi, Patrick Henry and Bob Bilheimer — toward whom I have developed a strong sense of theological and spiritual accountability.

One of the major problems in properly understanding pluralism as such is that we must take into account so many pluralisms these days — ethical, sexual, political, religious, theological, liturgical and others. No single evaluation covers all of these; there is no way of deciding for or against pluralism as such. To affirm the existing variety of Christian liturgies or political parties is one thing; it is quite another thing to affirm the existing variety of religions or sexual lifestyles. A theology of pluralism must take seriously the plurality of pluralisms.

The real challenge, of course, is to promote an appropriate pluralist sensitivity without slipping into an "anything-goes" relativism. The Bible offers encouragement. For example, the heavenly choir endorses an important many-ness when it sings the great eschatological hymn to the Lamb who shed his blood as a ransom for men and women "from every tribe and tongue and people and nation, and hast made them a kingdom and priests to our God" (Rev. 5:9).

It is precisely this vision of the culmination of God's plan, I am convinced, that provides the necessary spiritual resources for struggling creatively with the challenge of pluralism. Wheaton

College's Arthur Holmes has put it nicely: humility and hope, he observes, are two very important spiritual characteristics of the Christian's intellectual life. We know that only the Creator has a clear and comprehensive knowledge of all things; thus we are humble. But God has also promised eventually to lead us into that mode of perfect knowing that is proper to us as human creatures; thus we hope. These attitudes can give us a patience that can enable us to accept complexities and live with seemingly unconnected particularities without giving in to despair or cynicism.

There is no better way to cultivate the appropriate blend of humility and hope than to remind ourselves constantly of our Christian identity as participants in the Lamb's global network. A self-conscious awareness of our actual involvement in this complex community of rich particularities can induce us to keep talking together even when it seems like we have run up against ultimate pluralisms.

Someone said about my recent book, *Distorted Truth* (Harper & Row, 1989), that my comments on "the battle for the mind" struck him as a George Bush–like call for a kinder, gentler evangelicalism. I have no quarrel with that characterization — as long as we remember that kindness and gentleness already appear on the Apostle's list of the fruits of the Spirit in Galatians 5.

I do hope that evangelicals will become a kinder and gentler people in the coming decade. To appreciate better God's slowness is to see that we are living during the time of the divine patience, a long-suffering in which we are called to participate. Nor is the cultivation of patience, in both our personal lives and our public involvements, a mere temporary strategy, as John Murray Cuddihy seems to suggest when, in his excellent studies of the concept of civility, he advises Christians that the best way to gain a civil disposition is to postpone triumphalism until the eschaton. Kindness and gentleness are themselves the very stuff of eschatological existence. The ultimate triumph of sanctifying grace in our lives will occur only when we have learned not to grasp for a triumphalist spirit. The triumph that we await is not our triumph, but the victory of the Lamb before whom all our knees will bow and all of our tongues — including evangelical ones — will join in the larger ecumenical chorus that will declare that Jesus alone is Lord.

Evangelical involvement in the present public dialogue must be characterized by a kindness and gentleness that is fitting for creatures who are on their way to the eschaton. Not that there is no room for prophetic critique in our struggles with the crucial issues of contemporary human existence. But those corrective words must reflect our status as a people who have ourselves fled to the cross for healing and correction — and who, having received there some measure of repair, are emboldened to point others to the Source of the tender mercies that have touched our lives.

I begin the 1990s with a stronger sense than ever of the mystery of the divine majesty, as well as of the mystery of our own created complexity. But I also sense in myself a new enthusiasm for reflecting carefully on these profound mysteries.

Allan Boesak has often remarked that North Americans have a difficult time thinking theologically about apartheid. And that is unfortunate, says Boesak, since bad theology has contributed much to South Africa's problems and good theology is an important part of the solution. My move from a college philosophy department to a theological seminary is one expression of my conviction that Boesak is right. In fact, while considering recently whether to move into seminary administration, I heard one of the most convincing arguments from a friend, herself an academic administrator, who preached a fine little homily to me about administration being a very important context for thinking theologically about people and institutions.

These remarks construe the theological task rather broadly, of course. But that seems quite proper. My understanding of the scope of theological reflection continues to be guided by John Calvin's advice in the opening pages of his *Institutes:* the knowledge of God and the knowledge of our

human selfhood are intimately intertwined. Theological reflection requires that we relate all the information we have about
God to all that falls within the scope of human concern.

That is no easy assignment. But given my own most recent
assessments of the divine pace, I am convinced that we have
God's permission to take our time.

George A. Lindbeck

Confession and Community: An Israel-like View of the Church

I picture the process of change in my theological thinking in both archaeological and architectural terms: I have dug down into earlier layers of experience, and built on what went before. In my childhood and youth, I encountered cultural and religious groups other than my own; later I would engage them theologically, in reverse order. The Chinese were the first I knew as different, then Jews, Roman Catholics and non-Lutheran Protestants, in that sequence. The latter engaged my theological attention first, and then the Roman Catholics and Jews. The Chinese I have yet to examine theologically, and now that I am in my 60s, perhaps I never will. Their tacit influence on my thinking, however, lies deepest and it is only gradually that I have become aware of how pervasive it has been.

I was born in north central China, far from port cities and displays of Western power, and lived there for 17 years until shortly before Pearl Harbor. Because of illness I did not go away to boarding school until I was 12, and my life was very different

George A. Lindbeck is Pitkin Professor of Historical Theology at Yale University.

from the standard accounts of many Americans who grew up in the Far East, such as John Hersey. My parents were Swedish-American Lutheran missionaries who were more Sinicized than they realized. They contributed more than they knew to my childhood sense that the Chinese are the most intelligent, handsome and, at their Confucian best, cultivated of all peoples. To be sure, so my parents thought — they needed Christianity in order to make democracy work and escape communism, as well as for their souls' salvation, but that belief did not make me suppose that Westerners are superior. I came to think that apostate Christians were much worse than non-Christian Chinese, as the Nazis were proving. Thus China laid the groundwork for a disenchantment with Christendom that led me 30 years later to hope for the end of cultural Christianity as the enabling condition for the development of a diaspora Christianity. (Some articles I wrote in the '60s and '70s seem to me close to Stanley Hauerwas's position, but since then I have had reluctant second thoughts.)

Loyang, the city in which I was born and reared, was without electricity, running water, motorized transportation or even radios. The ways in which our neighbors lived and thought were as unmodern as those of the Han dynasty 2,000 years before. Further, famines, pestilences, brigandage and war (both civil and with the Japanese) engulfed our area repeatedly, and flight to safer places for short or long periods was common. Yet the processes and perceptions of life, I later came to think, were not greatly different from an American suburb, medieval ghetto or first-century Hellenistic household.

As I grew older I concluded that modernity is not unique in either its goodness or badness, but is just one epoch and culture among others, in some ways better and in some ways worse. Those who thought otherwise I found pretentious, including most of the writers of the past 400 years whose works were staple fare in my student days in Minnesota, Connecticut and France. Descartes, Hegel, Nietzsche, Heidegger, Sartre and Bultmann I found unappealing. Instead, I favored an unlikely combination of, on the one hand, medieval thinkers and their

33

contemporary interpreters such as Maritain and Gilson, and, on the other, the Reformers and their neoorthodox successors (who were fashionable) and confessional Lutherans (who were not). The only recent theologians I would now add to this list of major influences are Roman Catholics such as Rahner and von Balthasar. On the nontheological side I gained a new dimension in the '60s from Wittgensteinians, T. S. Kuhn, Peter Berger, Clifford Geertz and contemporary non-foundationalists. Whatever their differences, they are not bewitched by modern uniqueness: they hold that the basic processes of the linguistic, social and cognitive construction of reality and experience are much the same in all times and places, however varied the outcomes. One need not grow up in China to find such views persuasive, but in my case it helped.

The dichotomy I perceived between Chinese and non-Chinese was soon overlaid by a more salient trichotomy among Christians, non-Christians and Jews. By the time I was six or so, I saw these as the three basic types of human beings. That I would have noticed Jews is odd, for I had never, as far as I knew, met any, and my parents, products of the rural Midwest, probably hadn't either. The Old Testament, however, was as much a part of my upbringing as the New, and I early learned to think of the Jews as Jesus' people. Some of them, furthermore, had once lived in our part of China, and my father was fascinated by the remains of their T'ang dynasty settlements. Now other Jews from other parts of the world were returning to the Holy Land, as the Bible foretold. By 11, I was imaginatively a Darbyite Zionist daydreaming of becoming a kibbutz fighter. The rise of Nazism first made me aware of anti-Semitism. Some of the German missionaries we knew were at first pro-Hitler. Refugees began arriving in China, and two Jewish boys were members of my high school graduating class of 20.

My premillennialist philo-Semitism did not survive adolescence, but the aftereffects persisted. I was conditioned against Marcionite tendencies — evident in some post-Reformation Lutheranism — to spiritualize and privatize Christianity and neglect the Old Testament. I was also predisposed to welcome, at a much later date, the work of my Yale colleagues Brevard Childs and Hans Frei on canonical reading and on narrative and figural scriptural interpretation, respectively. More and more I have come to think that only the postcritical retrieval of such classic premodern hermeneutical strategies can give due weight to the abiding importance of Israel (including contemporary Judaism) and Israel's scriptures for Christians. This development in my thinking started late, beginning in the '70s, and first entered my published work in *The Nature of Doctrine* (1984). Now I am writing an ecclesiology that is in large part an "Israel-ology."

In contrast to my literary encounter with Jews, I knew Roman Catholics personally before I learned they were different. They were cousins, children of my mother's brother, whom we visited when on furlough in the States. Only gradually did I realize that theirs was the church that had persecuted Luther, slaughtered the innocents of whom I read in Foxe's *Book of Martyrs,* and supposedly taught that salvation was by works, not faith. I hoped that they trusted Jesus and not the pope's rules and regulations, but believed their chances of salvation would certainly be greater if they were Bible-believing Protestants.

The sad state of the Catholics troubled me in childhood, but not until I was in college did this concern translate into a theological and philosophical interest prompted by reading Gilson and Maritain. That interest led to doctoral work in medieval philosophy and theology as preparation for specialization in contemporary Catholicism. After ten years of teaching medieval thought at Yale (mostly in the philosophy department), I was selected by the Lutheran World Federation to be a delegated observer to the Second Vatican Council (1962-65), and since then have done most of my research and writing in the context of participation in national and international ecumenical dialogue, mostly with Roman Catholics. It is the ecumenical movement even more than my teaching at Yale (since Vatican II, all in the divinity school and the department of religious studies) that has been the context of my thinking.

My ecumenical concerns have been tilted in a Catholic direction. Under the influence of three European Lutherans, Kristin Skydsgaard, Peter Brunner and Edmund Schlink, and one American, Arthur Carl Piepkorn, I came to think that Lutheranism should try to become what it started out to be, a reform movement within the Catholic Church of the West. By such a strategy it can best contribute to the goal of wider Christian unity. This goal and strategy have guided almost all my work since then, though my notions of appropriate and feasible tactics have been changing in the past decade.

My turn away from developments in post-Reformation Protestantism started in midadolescence, years before my tilt toward Rome. In my early years I made no distinction between Lutherans and other Protestants. In order to maintain as much of a common Christian front as possible, American Lutherans in China, including my parents, did not advertise their confessional and sacramental differences from those to whom they were closest, Protestant conservative evangelicals (or "evangelicalists," as some Europeans call them). This was easy for them, for they were for the most part pietists of biblicistic and conversionist proclivities, but it confused me. Their pietism, which I confused with Lutheranism, early made me restive, not least because of my precocious reading of *Britannica* articles on evolution and Gibbon's *Decline and Fall* (my father's library was short on comic books). My restiveness was increased by memorizing Luther's *Small Catechism* for confirmation, and by arguments in boarding school with, for example, Southern Baptist classmates about such matters as infant baptism. Obviously Lutherans were different from other Protestants (that was a relief), but I still did not know what they were: I was looking for an identity.

That was provided in my sophomore and junior years by a new headmaster, Pastor Albue, a bright, personable and athletic young missionary, the idol of the high school students. He alerted me to the possibility of an unambiguously confessional Lutheranism that was devout but not pietistic, and quite unreticent about baptismal regeneration and the real presence.

Others whom I came to know during the same period pointed in the same direction, most notably the Norwegian missionary scholar K. L. Reichelt, suspected of heresy by evangelicals because of his immense knowledge of and respect for Buddhism, but remembered by me for his Lutheran preaching.

Through such influences, I began to opt for a Reformation Christianity self-consciously opposed to modern Protestantism in both its conservative and liberal forms. Its starting point is neither biblicistic nor experientialist, and certainly not individualistic, but dogmatic: it commences with the historic Christian communal confession of faith in Christ. For the Reformers, as for the Orthodox and Catholic churches of East and West, that confession is the one expressed in the ancient trinitarian and christological creeds. The Reformers did not so much try to prove these creeds from Scripture (and certainly not from experience), but rather read Scripture in their light, and then used the Bible thus construed to mold experience and guide thought and action. God's word, in their premodern hermeneutics, was ever applicable, and changed in import with the circumstances. It was not constrained to a single kind of meaning by inerrantist theories of inspiration or liberal ones of revelatory experience. My understanding of the implications of beginning with dogma has developed greatly (see *The Nature of Doctrine*), but not the creedal and confessional starting point. That has remained the integrating center of my later theological work.

Although I early defined myself theologically in opposition to modern Protestantism (rather than in dialogue, as with Roman Catholicism, Judaism and China), I have constantly been preoccupied with Protestants. I have lived with conservative Protestants in my youth, and liberal ones ever since I arrived at Yale as a student over 40 years ago. I keep hoping that evangelicals will not think my work compromises their emphases on the love of Jesus and on biblical authority, and that liberals will not suppose it is inconsistent with intellectual openness or commitment to peace and justice. The desire to communicate affects theology, and changes I have perceived in the climate of discourse have affected my thinking in recent years.

The most important change for my work in the past 20 years is the increasing polarization between the modern right and left in both Protestantism and Catholicism, and the corresponding decline of a center rooted in premodern communal traditions. That center had been constituted by the Protestant neo-orthodoxy and Catholic *nouvelle théologie,* which were ascending from the 1920s to the 1960s. They had sought renewal in the light of contemporary needs by critically returning to the sources of the faith in Scripture and premodern tradition. They failed, on the whole, to escape the limitations of modern historical criticism and, with partial exceptions, did not retrieve premodern classic hermeneutics. Yet they provided the context for the flourishing in Protestantism and Catholicism of the unitive ecumenism that has been my life's work.

Now, however, interest has shifted more and more to unmediated *aggiornamento,* the updating of faith and practice by direct translation into presumably more intelligible and relevant modern idioms and actions. This is a revival of the liberal strategy, familiar since the Enlightenment, of letting the world set the church's agenda. What is different is chiefly the agenda and the tactics, for the world has changed. The dechristianization of the public realm proceeds apace, and communal traditions have weakened. The ecumenical focus has shifted from church unity, from reconciling the historic communities, to the service of the world, and therefore away from the kind of ecumenism that has been my chief concern. The new left is more extreme than the old, and is stronger in the historically mainline churches than ever before.

The extremism and the strength of the right is also increasing. Rightists also are unconcerned with church unity and community or with *ressourcement.* They emphasize not the critical retrieval of the sources of the faith but recent traditions formed in earlier modern contexts. Roman Catholic traditionalists cling to a 19th-century version of Tridentism and, judging by Archbishop Marcel Lefebvre and his followers, are more schismatic than the progressives. Protestant evangelicals are also fixated on the 19th century and are systematically antiecumenical. After the interlude between the 1920s and '60s, the polarization between right and left characteristic of modern mass societies is on the rise and swamping the churches as never before.

Others share this picture of the present situation, but I find it less depressing than most for both nontheological and theological reasons. The four centuries of modernity are coming to an end. Its individualistic foundational rationalism, always wavering between skeptical relativism and totalitarian absolutism, is being replaced, as I earlier mentioned, by an understanding of knowledge and belief as socially and linguistically constituted. Ideologies rooted in Enlightenment rationalism are collapsing. This is unmistakably true of the leftist ones after the *annus mirabilis* 1989, but it is also true of liberal democratic capitalism on the right. Politically pragmatic liberalism may be practically necessary in pluralistic societies, but as an individualistic secular ideology it is no more viable in the long run than its illiberal counterparts. Societies need strong mediating communities through which traditions of personal virtue, common good and ultimate meaning are transmitted to new generations. It is hard to see how such communities can flourish without a religious dimension, and in traditionally Christian lands, that means a Christian one.

I once welcomed the passing of Christendom and found Richard John Neuhaus's demurrers misplaced; but now, as I earlier mentioned, I am having uncomfortable second thoughts. The waning of cultural Christianity might be good for the churches, but what about society? To my chagrin, I find myself thinking that traditionally Christian lands when stripped of their historic faith are worse than others. They become unworkable or demonic. There is no reason to suppose that what happened in Nazi Germany cannot happen in liberal democracies, though the devils will no doubt be disguised very differently. From this point of view, the Christianization of culture can be in some situations the churches' major contribution to feeding the poor, clothing the hungry and liberating the imprisoned. So it was in the past and, given the disintegration of modern ideologies, so it may be at times in the future. Talk of "Christian America" and John Paul II's vision of a "Christian Europe" make me uncomfortable, but I have seen a number of totally unexpected improbabilities come to pass in my lifetime, such as Roman Catholic transformations and communism's collapse, and cannot rule these out as impossible.

Whether or not re-Christianization occurs, however, our era is a new one, and the churches are in the midst of a vast transformation. My understanding of what is needed has developed in three interrelated directions in the past decade: hermeneutical, organizational and ecclesiological. Renewal depends, I have come to think, on the spread of proficiency in premodern yet postcritical Bible reading, on restructuring the churches into something like pre-Constantinian organizational patterns, and on the development of an Israel-like understanding of the church.

These elements belong together. For classic hermeneutics, the Hebrew bible is the basic ecclesiological textbook. Christians see themselves within those texts, when read in the light of Christ, as God's people, chosen for service not preferment, and bound together in a historically and sociologically continuous community that God refuses to disown whether it is faithful or unfaithful, united or disunited, in the catacombs or on the throne. It was in some such way as this that the Christians of the first centuries, whom we call catholic, used Israel's story as a template for their own existence. It was they, not the Marcionite or gnostic Christians, who developed a communal life strong enough to become the great majority and win the Empire, despite their lack of social, economic, intellectual, political or military power.

They were also, however, supersessionists who claimed to have replaced Israel, thus denying that the Jews were any longer, except negatively, God's chosen people; and they were triumphal-

40

ists who believed that the church could not be unfaithful as Israel had been. The logic of Christian faith thereby became perversely opposed in a variety of ways to the fundamental belief in Jesus as the crucified Messiah. It has taken the disasters of Christian apostasy, often disguised as orthodoxy, in combination with historical-critical work to unmask the problems. We can now see that the early Christian errors resulted from self-serving gentile Christian misappropriations of intra-Jewish polemics over Jesus' messiahship, and that these errors are blatantly opposed to much of the New Testament witness, especially Paul's. But if these errors are rejected, so I have come to think, Christians can now apply Israel's story to themselves without supersessionism or triumphalism. The story's power is undiminished. "Oneness in Christ" gains a concrete specificity that it otherwise lacks. All Christians, whether Catholics, Protestants and Orthodox or African, American and Chinese, belong to a single community of morally imperative responsibility for one another like the members of the early church or contemporary Jews.

These are the issues with which I am now struggling. I think I can show that none of the major Christian traditions is dogmatically opposed to an Israel-like view of the church, but acceptance of it involves a break with nearly 2,000 years of both modern and premodern Christian self-understandings. Unitive ecumenism, among other things, needs to be reconceived. It can no longer be thought of, as I have done most of my life, as a matter of reconciling relatively intact and structurally still-Constantinian communions from the top down. Rather it must be thought of as reconstituting Christian community and unity from, so to speak, the bottom up. It is here that the structuring of the church in the first centuries is especially instructive. The ecumenical journey when thus conceived will be longer but also more adventurous: renewal and unification become inseparable.

This focus on building Christian community will seem outrageous to some in view of the world's needs, but it is a strength for those who see the weakening of communal commitments and loyalties as modernity's fundamental disease.

Perhaps no greater contribution to peace, justice and the environment is possible than that provided by the existence of intercontinental and interconfessional communal networks such as the churches already are to some extent, and can become more fully, if God wills.

By centering this article on communities, I have not mentioned, for example, those who taught me most about *how* — as distinct from *what* — to think theologically and historically: Robert L. Calhoun and H. Richard Niebuhr of Yale, and Paul Vignaux of Paris. Nor have I mentioned my daughter, a Christian student of rabbinics, from whom I have learned much about Judaism; nor my wife, a Presbyterian and professor of religious studies, who has in various ways greatly heightened my appreciation of Calvin. Yet the communal focus, though oversimple, is not wrong. As far as my scholarly career is concerned, I have always been primarily interested in how ideas function in communal traditions of language and practice rather than in themselves or in their role in individual lives considered in isolation.

I seem to have come nearly full circle. The ecclesiology on which I am working concerns Chinese, Jews, Roman Catholics and Protestants within the horizon of a crumbling of modernity that brings Christians closer to premodernity than they've been in perhaps 300 years, and closer to the situation of the first centuries than they've been in more than a millennium and a half. We are now better placed than perhaps ever before to retrieve, critically and repentantly, the heritage in the Hebrew scriptures, apostolic writings and early tradition. This retrieval is also more urgent than ever if the churches are to become the kind of global and ecumenical community that the new age needs. Such are the convictions that now inform my thinking, and they are developments rather than departures from my early experiences and youthful theology. Archaeology and architecture almost coincide.

Elizabeth Achtemeier

Renewed Appreciation for an Unchanging Story

My mind has not changed a great deal, because the biblical story has not changed. The account is still there, from countless witnesses, of God's thrusts into history. God created his world to be "very good," but we corrupted his creation by attempting to be our own gods and goddesses and by trying to shape our own futures apart from him. We thereby brought distortion and ruin into the world of nature, family, work and community, bringing upon ourselves God's absence and curse, and the sentence of eternal death.

But God would not give up on us. He called Abraham and Sarah out of Mesopotamia to be the forebears of a new community that would live under his guiding lordship in justice, righteousness and obedience. Then through all of the vicissitudes of actual life in the ancient Near East, God made himself a people from those forebears — delivering them from slavery in Egypt, protecting them against their enemies, leading them through the terrors of the wilderness, entering into covenant

---

Elizabeth Achtemeier is adjunct professor of Bible and homiletics at Union Theological Seminary in Richmond, Virginia.

with them, giving them his guiding presence in the covenant law, bringing them into a land flowing with milk and honey, giving them a Davidic king to be their protector of justice in peace and in war, and finally taking up his own dwelling in their temple on the Mount of Zion.

When that people nevertheless rebelled against God's rule, he constantly wept and worried over them, repeatedly forgiving their waywardness and sending them prophets to speak his words of judgment and mercy. Then to erase their sin he sent them into exile, but he nevertheless promised them "a future and a hope," forgiveness and blessing in a new land, with a new covenant written on their hearts, under a new Davidic king ruling over an obedient, faithful and righteous community of all peoples.

Finally, in the fullness of time, God kept his promise to Israel, sending his Son to be the cornerstone, covenant and Davidic leader of that new, forgiven, universal community. Through the death and resurrection of that Son, God wiped out our sinful past, joined us to himself in an everlasting and unbreakable covenant, gave us instructions about how to live until his Son comes again to set up his rule over all the earth, and promised, to all who trust his ways and work, eternal life and joy in his kingdom which will have no end.

That biblical story is the bedrock of my faith and the faith of my church, and always I, with my church, am called to hear that history and respond to it, pass it on and live by its promise. Yet, events in our changing and torturous times constantly illumine new portions of the story and call for new responses to it, just as they also call for new reflection and understanding. In the past 20 years, new emphases from the biblical history have impressed themselves upon me in response first of all to the fruits of the '60s.

In June of 1989 the *Philadelphia Inquirer* printed portions of an interview with Timothy Leary, "the world's most famous acid head." "It's true," Leary was quoted as saying, "that in the '60s we were young, romantic, naïve and sometimes obnoxious.

But we were right. I regret nothing." The truth is, we have a lot to regret, and indeed, a lot of which to repent. In the '60s our society decided that drugs were acceptable, that sex was free and that authorities were useless. "The old taboos are dead or dying," exulted *Newsweek* in 1967. "The people are breaking the bonds of puritan society and helping America to grow up." We are now paying the price of that blind and irresponsible folly — in a drug war that we are not winning, in burgeoning crime that has made city neighborhoods uninhabitable, in teenage pregnancies and "children having children," in rampant abortions, swelling welfare roles, sexually transmitted diseases, self-indulgent neglect of community good, and countless ruined lives. We chose our own way and as with the primal choice in the garden of Eden, we brought on ourselves the way of death.

In the light of that, I therefore have come to a new appreciation of the place of law and commandment in the gospel, in both Old and New Testaments. Obedience to the divine law does not form the basis of our relationship with God, but is rather the outcome of it. God redeems us by the cross and resurrection before we have done any deed and while we are yet sinners. But having made us his own, God does not abandon us to wander in the dark. Instead, he gives us commandments as guides in this new life he has given us. "This is the way," he says to us, "Walk in it."

God's guidance in the new life is pure grace, given out of his love for us. Heaven knows our society is unable to instruct us about how to live the Christian life; society is still lost in the willfulness of its own sinful ways and knows nothing of God's way. Apart from God's continuing guidance, we do not know how to live. But God, in his incredible mercy, wants it "to go well with us," as Deuteronomy puts it. God wants us to have abundant life. God wants us to have joy. And so in love he gives us directions to point the way to wholeness, life and joy.

Sometimes, of course, we do not like the directions. For example, God says, "You shall not commit adultery," while almost every program on TV assures us that it is the only way to go. But seeing the consequences in our society — two out of every three marriages now end in divorce — I am overwhelmed daily by the love of God manifested in his commandment. Truly he is a God who wants us to have the unsurpassed joy that comes from a lifelong, faithful marital commitment. Experiencing that joy and the blessing that results from obedience to other commandments as well, I have come to a new appreciation of the wisdom and mercy embodied in the divine instructions given us in the Scriptures.

Similarly, I think I have come to a new understanding of the place of sanctification in the Christian life, perhaps mainly because the doctrine of sanctification has fallen into disuse in so many churches in our culture. Who in our society want to be *good* anymore? Persons strive to be self-fulfilled, integrated, successful, even rich, beautiful and thin, but rarely does one find a person who wants to be *good* as the Bible defines it. Who speaks of "a man or woman of God," or of a Christlike person? Yet the New Testament tells us that that is God's goal for us, and that he is changing his faithful people into the image of Christ "from one degree of glory to another."

I have encountered persons undergoing that process of sanctification in my travels throughout the church, and they are in fact lights in the darkness of our world, savory salt and leaven in the loaf — persons who have become so saturated with the will of God that one could entrust anything to them. I cannot but think that they are the forerunners of what the church as a whole is supposed to be — a beachhead on the shores of this present wilderness, a little colony of heaven, set into the jungle that is our world to claim its territory for God's rule over it.

Such persons of God inspire me to follow after them, but they also impress upon me that the way of Christ is a discipline — of prayer, of regular worship and study of the Scriptures, of constant willing after obedience to God. Self-fulfillment and individual freedom are claimed as inalienable rights in our society, but persons undergoing sanctification know that holiness comes from having a master. Israel lost her life when she refused to wear a yoke, Jeremiah says. Similarly, our Lord taught us that life comes from bearing a cross that does away with self, and the sanctified life results from accepting Christ's blessed yoke. "Take my yoke upon you, and learn of me," is Christ's instruction, for that yoke is easy and that burden is light and that discipline leads to rest for our souls.

Indeed, I have come to understand more and more that it is only by wearing the yoke of Christ and following his guiding reins that we have that perfect freedom for which so many long in our society. Our difficulty in America these days is that we want freedom without discipline, rights without responsibilities, self-fulfillment without the necessity of committing ourselves. How often do we leave off the first phrase of Jesus' teaching: "*If you are my disciples,* you shall know the truth, and the truth shall make you free"? But freedom comes only with commitment, and commitment to Christ is the only truth.

We sometimes kid ourselves into thinking that we can be free just for and of ourselves. But the apostle Paul tells us that we are either slaves to sin or slaves to Christ. There is no neutral ground between those two bonds. And it is in that bondage to Christ, as he is portrayed for us in the Scriptures, that I have been instructed more and more in his freedom. What liberty he gives us when we bind ourselves to the Word!

I think this has become ever clearer to me as I have observed the growth and course of church bureaucracies in the past three decades. For some reason — and I do not posit a necessary correlation — the more church membership declines, the larger become the ecclesiastical bureaucracies — those bodies that the late Paul Ramsey aptly named "the church-and-society *curia*," those bodies that seem to have a disturbing way of following the latest media-generated fad and that are sure they know the course the church should follow better than do the people in the pews. Such *curia* seem to have no freedom from the society around them, even though they claim to be prophetic voices in the church. Rather, they have rather well-defined ideologies, of either the left or the right, and therefore rather predictable positions on public issues.

But rarely it is through being saturated by the word of God — getting it into one's bones until one sees everything through its values, reason, language and worldview — that we are given true freedom from the society around us and no longer need be "blown about by every wind of doctrine." That is the freedom one sees in the prophets — the freedom of a Jeremiah to preach treason when the Babylonians are at the gate, or the freedom of an Elijah to topple a royal dynasty for the sake of one little vineyard next to the palace, or indeed the freedom of a Nathan to turn around and support an adulterous Bathsheba, his former enemy. The freedom of the prophets comes from the word of God burning in their bones, just as Paul says that when we are "in Christ," we no longer see any- thing from "a human point of view." That is true freedom, and more and more I have come to realize that it is the only rock in the midst of the turbulent waters of our rushing times.

Similarly, I have come ever more to realize that the only freedom from one's sinful self lies in that liberty given us by Christ. This has been impressed upon me by observing the women's movement in the church. Certainly, the women have a just cause, because they have been discriminated against as second class members in the church for centuries, despite the Lord's and the earliest New Testament churches' clear example to the contrary. Women graduates at Union Seminary in Virginia, most of whom are topnotch preachers and pastors, still have difficulty finding a call to a pulpit. If the church had lived up to its gospel, in which we are all one in Christ Jesus, we would not be in our feminist mess today.

But many contemporary feminists in the church have un- fortunately concentrated everything around themselves. They have made their experience the ultimate authority, above the Scriptures. Their liberation has become their all-consuming occupation, coloring everything they write, say and do. The radicals among them have even begun to claim that they have a goddess in themselves, or that they are divine, because they have substituted for the biblical God a "Primal Matrix" or "Mother Goddess" or great world spirit flowing in and through all things and people. Mistaking Christ's "dying to self" as a ploy to keep them oppressed, they have elevated themselves to the place of the divine and thus denied themselves any knowledge of the glorious liberty of the children of God. That surely is captivity to sin and bondage to one's feeble, mortal person. And such captivity leads only to death, whereas God in Christ so much desires to give us only abundant life.

Many in the church *curia* have almost totally surrendered to such ways of death, perhaps from a sense of guilt over the past treatment of females or from a real sense of justice, but often without thought or theological understanding of the consequences. And so the rest of the church may find its liturgy changed by some worship committee into a celebration of a Canaanite, fertility birthing god, or it may discover that it is no longer allowed to sing a hymn based on Isaiah 63. At the same time, the church is told by feminists that its Scriptures, the only written guarantees of its freedom in Christ, are now suspect and to be judged as true only if they accord with modern feminist views. Alongside the body of Christ, some feminists are constructing a new church, called women-church, and celebrating a new religion, sometimes utilizing the symbol of a female "Christa" on a cross. It is difficult to imagine any more confining bondage to one's sinful self and society.

In the tenth and ninth centuries B.C., Israel in the Old Testament was tempted to construct a new culture and a new religion based on Canaanite models. The parallels with our society are many and ominous. And it was only the early, non-writing prophets, such as Elijah, Elisha and Micaiah ben Imla, who preserved the nature of the Mosaic covenant faith before the threat of total corruption by pagan religion and culture. God grant us a new prophetic voice in our time, perhaps rising up in protest from the pews, or sounding forth, as did Karl Barth, from an obscure and seemingly unimportant pulpit, a prophetic voice that proclaims justice and equality for women, but on the sure basis of the authority of the Bible and the equalizing nature of the apostolic Christian faith.

This brings me to my last point. Through 30 years of teaching in seminaries I have become convinced that the church has largely failed in its mission of educating its people in the apostolic, biblical faith. Every preacher who enters a pulpit these days must assume that the congregation knows almost nothing about the content of the Scriptures. The language of faith, the meaning of the sacraments and the basic doctrines of the Christian church are almost totally devoid of meaning for the average churchgoer. Thus our congregations are often at the mercy of the latest kooky cult (witness Shirley MacLaine and New Age religion), and there is no common biblical story that binds them together in their faith. Individuals drift from one church to another, without roots, without religious history, without any Rock or Refuge or any sense that they belong to a communion of saints or participate in an ongoing history of salvation that God is working out in their lives and world.

One could blame such biblical and doctrinal illiteracy on several factors. Surely the fact that most children remain in the Sunday worship service only long enough for the children's sermon has deprived them of the opportunity of learning the language of liturgy and prayer and of absorbing the content of doctrine from hymn and from sermon. It is no wonder that the church is losing its young people; the formative years of their childhood were spent in another room. Surely too, despite our multimedia and high-gloss curricula with pictures, Christian training has been occupied more often with relevance, social issues and entertainment than it has with learning (and even memorizing) the content of the biblical message.

But in the last analysis, I cannot help thinking that our Christian illiteracy is due largely to a failure of the pulpit. The Christian faith was passed on for centuries, long before we had educational programs and Sunday schools, from one generation to another by its preachers from their pulpits. Yet far too many clergy today hand over educational matters to associates and religious educators, while they themselves dispense therapy, psychology and the latest religious or social opinions.

I gave a talk some years ago in which I mentioned that the Christian faith was a matter of life and death. Afterwards, I was approached by a publisher who found that statement so amazing that he asked me if I would care to write a book about it. Surely his amazement was symptomatic of our society's sickness: that it knows no divine commandment nor desires any sanctification; that it seeks life apart from God, who is the sole source of life; that it searches for freedom but is unwilling to bear a cross; that it wants a story to live by, but will not teach or learn the One Story. Those are, indeed, all matters of life and death, and the church must deal with them if it truly wants to be the Body of Christ, and a light to the world and salt and leaven.

Richard John Neuhaus

Religion and Public Life:
The Continuing Conversation

Thirty years ago, when I was 23 and trying to situate myself in a confusing world, I determined to be, in descending order of importance, religiously orthodox, culturally conservative, politically liberal and economically pragmatic. That quadrilateral still serves.

As far back as I can remember, it seemed to me necessary to situate oneself, to define oneself, to take a position. The usual psychological scheme has it that the securities of childhood are shattered by adolescence and then, in adulthood, one puts together the pieces of the world and one's place in it. My first and most enduring experience, however, was of a world all in pieces. It is not that I had an unhappy childhood; not at all.

Rather, my earliest impressions were that reality was terrifying, meanings seemed arbitrary and all was threatened by chaos and death. Heavy stuff for a kid, one might think. But it

---

Richard John Neuhaus is director of Religion and Public Life, a research and education institute in New York City, and editor in chief of First Things: A Monthly Journal of Religion and Public Life.

struck me also as being like a game. Taking positions was a way of imposing order on reality, and letting reality test the order imposed. Admittedly, that might make one argumentative, and so I suppose I have always been, to the unhappiness of some and the delight of others. But the right word for this thrusting and testing is conversation, and, "coming to myself in the middle of the journey of life," I am pleased to report that what Dante called the "dark wood" seems to recede ever farther into the past.

Of the four positions in my quadrilateral, "politically liberal" has most changed over these 30 years. People frequently claim that it is the world that has changed, while they have remained true to their principles. Frequently that is true. But of course I have changed, recognizing the wisdom of Cardinal Newman's observation that to live is to change, and to be perfect is to have changed often. On the other hand, Lutherans do not believe in perfectionism, and I am, in fact, struck much more by the continuities than by the discontinuities in my thinking. I am aware that not everybody sees it that way.

Many assert that I was a liberal, even a radical, in the '60s and that I am now a neoconservative. In 1956 Will Herberg wrote that Reinhold Niebuhr, in his neoorthodox turn from political utopianism, represented the "new conservatism" in American intellectual life. Conservative liberalism is the better term — and the analogy with Niebuhr should not be pressed — but what Herberg meant by the "new conservatism" of 1956 is the neoconservatism of today. In my own case, I can be quite specific about the transmogrifications of liberalism that made it increasingly problematic to call myself simply a liberal.

From 1961 to 1978 I lived and worked in the black worlds of Brooklyn. Intensely engaged in the civil rights movement under the leadership of Martin Luther King, Jr., I first broke with the left when "black power" emerged in 1965. My sympathies were entirely with Dr. King and against the racial separatism that became the radical chic embraced by many friends and allies. Authentic liberalism, I still believe, opposes the group stereotyping, quota systems and reverse discriminations that have trashed the dream voiced by Dr. King at the March on Washington in August 1963. The promise of community and moral redemption has largely been replaced by the fashionable angers of separatism, victimization and ideologized resentment.

In the later '60s I was also deeply involved in the war on poverty. Slowly and painfully I came to see how well-intended programs were contributing to the corruption and dependency of the poor that would result in what is now recognized as a radically isolated black underclass, a new and ominous development in American life. I am gratified to see signs of increased attention to the "mediating structures" paradigm by which social policy can be built on the potentials rather than the pathologies of poor communities.

Another important year was 1967, when I published in *Commonweal* "Abortion: The Dangerous Assumptions." I would still argue that the protection of the unborn and other vulnerable human life is the liberal cause, for liberalism's goal is an ever more inclusive definition of the community for which we accept common responsibility. Abortion is about more than abortion: it is about the severely handicapped, the helpless aged, the hopelessly deranged, and all the expendable others who cannot pass the "quality of life" tests imposed by the strong. I firmly believe that someday many who now call themselves liberal will bitterly regret having endorsed a lethal logic and practice that is premised upon the survival of the fittest.

Breaking ranks with the left over abortion, I experienced the illiberality of certain liberalisms. Its wrath was impressive. My dissent from the party line clearly made me a security risk in the eyes of some in The Movement — that exhilaratingly conflicted concatenation of impulses toward a radically new and better world. Nonetheless, I still belonged to the "us" that defined itself against "them." In 1969 I could still represent the radical position against Peter Berger's conservatism in our book *Movement and Revolution,* even if the gravamen of my argument was a caution against careless revolutionisms.

I made further steps away from the political orthodoxy of the left. In 1968, for instance, at the Chicago Democratic convention I was a Eugene McCarthy delegate who had hoped to support Robert Kennedy. With other delegates who protested Mayor Richard J. Daley's martial law, I sat in a jail cell listening to the broadcast of Hubert Humphrey's acceptance speech invoking the peace of St. Francis. Chicago marked the point at which The Movement was irretrievably captured by the counterculture of pharmaceutical mysticism, polymorphous perversity and the media-seeking antics of such as Abbie Hoffman and his Chicago Seven. Montgomery, Selma, King and the two Kennedys were being relegated to a distant and irrelevant past. For a cultural conservative, the "Woodstock Nation" was nothing to celebrate. That may seem like the rueful rumination of one who at 32 had arrived at premature middle age, but it is my reflection on the lost dignity of liberalism. As they drew to a close, the '60s were being turned into a moral slum of a decade.

The Vietnam War occasioned another break between me and the left. In 1965 Daniel Berrigan, Abraham Joshua Heschel and I started Clergy Concerned About Vietnam (later Clergy and Laity Concerned). Half a year after Hanoi's victory in 1975, Jim Forest of the Fellowship of Reconciliation and I drafted a protest against the brutal oppression and massive violation of human rights in Vietnam. We thought that we who had opposed the war had an obligation to care about the consequences of our "success." Many in The Movement disagreed. Of the 104 national leaders of the antiwar effort whom we asked to join in our protest, 51 refused, declaring, in effect, that there could be no enemies to the left. Churchpeople with whom I had often marched visited Vietnam and returned to praise the humanity of the new regime. I knew about the Western dupes of Stalin in the 1930s, of course, but this was my first experience of liberals as apologists for oppression. It would not, regrettably, be my last.

Our political culture and our churches are still sorting out "the lessons of Vietnam." One lesson I hope I have learned is the necessity of attending to consequences. On both the right and the left, political discourse is too often marked by moral recklessness. Many think the important thing is to take the "correct" position, and let the devil take the consequences. As often as not, he does. During the war our opponents warned about the bloodbath that would follow U.S. withdrawal. We dismissively responded that nothing could be worse than the war itself. We were wrong. By any honest measure of injustice and suffering — the rivers of blood and mounds of corpses, the reeducation camps and the killing fields of Cambodia, the millions of boat people at the bottom of the China Sea or languishing in refugee hovels to this day — what followed was worse than what went before. Much worse. I am familiar with, and unconvinced by, contorted arguments that America is primarily to blame for the aftermath of the war as well.

I do not say we were wrong to oppose the war. For a number of reasons, some of them not the ones usually given, I can argue that we were right to oppose the war. During those years my chief intellectual antagonist was the late Paul Ramsey of Princeton. He did not so much defend the justice of the war as he challenged the reasoning of those who were so sure of its injustice. The extent to which my opposition to the war was honest was due in very large part to Paul Ramsey. And it was due to long and difficult arguments with my two brothers, both of whom served two tours in Vietnam. And it was due to the young black men of Brooklyn who fought there, some of whom died there, whom I was not prepared to say had died in vain or in support of an evil cause. Let no one judge before the time (I Cor. 4:5).

It did not take much courage to protest the war. I remember with shame how often I failed to correct those who said I was heroic and prophetic in leading demonstrations and going to jail from time to time. The price of protest was a self-chosen inconvenience, and the reward was minor celebrity. We were not heroes, never mind prophets. At the time, and more strongly in retrospect, it seemed to me that the rot of moral conceit was far advanced in The Movement. A large part of a generation thinks it earned its moral credentials in that protest and is deeply threatened by the thought that those credentials could be questioned. While that fear is understandable, we should not give in to it. The result of my own questioning is that I do not think that we were wrong to oppose the war, but I am very sure that we were neither so right nor so righteous as we thought we were. I will not be surprised if, on this question at the Great Assize, Paul Ramsey will have less to answer for than I.

It is passing strange that we in the Christian community, which proclaims the inexhaustible mercy of God, fear admitting our mistakes and confessing our sins. I recognize this in myself and must constantly remember that we can act in the courage of our uncertainties only because forgiveness is the final certainty. It is also strange that many find candor most difficult with respect to their political positionings and posturings. Part of the imperiousness of the political in our culture is that our identities are so tied to our politics. I am increasingly convinced that the churches' chief political contribution is to debunk the inflated importance of politics. Only then can those who are called to it get on with the modest and ever-ambiguous task of politics.

Tragically, church leaders across the spectrum too often succumb to the lie that politics is "the real world" to which all else is instrumental. The "equipment of the saints" (Eph. 4) has been replaced by the recruitment of saints to our favored causes. Twenty-five years ago I thought Jacques Ellul's warning against "the political illusion" constituted a brake upon political commitment. Now I see it as a counsel of freedom from political corruption. Twenty-five years ago I criticized the Lutheran "two kingdoms" concept because it denied redemptive significance to politics. Now I embrace it as one of the best ways, if not the best way, of avoiding the perilous confusion and fatal conflation of the City of God and the City of Man.

In short, I am increasingly formed and informed by the radical wisdom of Augustine. It follows that I am increasingly unimpressed by the incessant claims that for Christians the great issues at the end of the 20th century are substantively different from those posed at the beginning of the fifth. Our enthusiasm for the new is jointly driven by ignorance and the bad faith that refuses to acknowledge its debts. "Tradition," Chesterton famously said, "is the democracy of the dead," and we in ordered ministry are most particularly called to do our duty by the dead, knowing that in Christ they live.

Even more than I did before, I believe we also have a duty to nurture and enhance another democracy, what we call liberal democracy, as it is exemplified, however imperfectly, in the American experiment. Today, as at other times in history, varieties of left and right converge in their hostility to liberal democracy. Liberationists on the left and theocratic reconstructionists on the right agree in their disdain for the greatest political achievement of modernity, which is liberal democracy. Driven by an essentially monistic hunger, neither party can abide democratic pluralism. John Courtney Murray allowed that pluralism, while it may not be God's will, seems to be written into the script of history. My hunch is that pluralism is God's will for history until the End Time. Spelling out what that might mean is among the tasks of theology and political theory awaiting the next generation.

Having written ten books, edited more than a dozen others and published hundreds of articles, I have to date left a paper trail of shameless proportions. I sometimes sympathize with Karl Kraus, the prolific Viennese critic who, when asked why he wrote books, answered that he had not enough character not to write books. But I would like to think that my writing is not a way of settling disputes or scoring points but a matter of continuing the conversation, of traditioning the tradition.

Conversation means, among other things, working hard at engaging significant differences. I sometimes think that Religion and Public Life, the institute I work for in New York, is one of the few truly ecumenical agencies in the country. Through conferences, consultations, research projects and publications we work assiduously at involving Roman Catholic, evangelical, fundamentalist, Jewish and, to be sure, old-line church leaders in the culture-forming tasks religion performs in public life. At the risk of offending, I suggest that the old-line churches that lay historical claim to being ecumenical are today frequently the most insular and defensive. Those accustomed to calling for dialogue have become curiously monological. This is very sad, and we must hope it is not beyond remedy.

Although many missed the point, and perhaps it was not made clearly enough, my book *The Naked Public Square* is a plea for the old-line to resume its rightful role in shaping our public moral discourse. But it seems to me that the several worlds of the old-line continue to be dominated by sentimental moralism, strident utopianism and self-pitying complaints that their "prophetic" witness is unappreciated, all orchestrated by church managers who are refugees from radicalisms past. I hope this is a passing phase. Yet for the present and the foreseeable future the leadership in religion's culture-forming tasks has passed to evangelicals and Roman Catholics, and to a younger community of Jewish scholars who are thinking in fresh ways about the place of biblical faith in the American experiment.

As with the quadrilateral I mentioned at the start I have been well served by variations on a theme that I long ago stole from Paul Tillich. It is that politics is in largest part an expression of culture, and at the heart of culture is religion. And at the heart of religion are the truth claims that define religion's "construction of reality," to use Berger's phrase. This brings us to the role of theology as such. As a second-order enterprise, theology reflects on those truth claims and the experience of the community gathered and sustained by those claims. As a first-order enterprise, theology finds its chief end in the chief end of man. And that chief end, as stated with unsurpassed excellence by the smaller Westminster Catechism, is to glorify God and enjoy him forever.

This insistently antiutilitarian understanding of theology informed my part in the 1975 Hartford Appeal for Theological

Affirmation. As some readers may recall, that document urged a revived understanding of transcendence. In a frustrating but not unamusing turn, sundry liberationisms, led by the feminist variety, now contend that, since God is so very transcendent, no language is adequate to talk about the divine reality or purpose (which is true), and that we are therefore free to use whatever language best meets what we define as our needs (which is false). I believe that the Hartford Appeal is more pertinent today than it was 15 years ago. What Hartford cautioned against as a danger is today widely embraced as a virtue. If pleasure is permitted where he is now, Ludwig Feuerbach must be pleased as he surveys the contemporary theological scene with its endemic confusions and conflations of utility and truth. He might be surprised, however, to see how theology has not only survived but flourished after agreeing with him that its "truths" are but the projections of human needs and aspirations. Much of what is called Christian theology today has with remarkable aplomb taken the death of God in stride. The Christian gospel is as much in eclipse today as it was in, say, 1517.

I take that gospel to be what the Reformation said it is: God's justifying the godless by grace through faith because of Jesus Christ. There are other ways of formulating it, but that is the gist of the matter. In my theological understanding of the Christian reality, I am indebted to innumerable men and women. In eclectic fashion, I have no doubt taken thoughts from each and turned them in directions that they probably did not intend and might not approve. But the two to whom I am most indebted are Arthur Carl Piepkorn and Wolfhart Pannenberg. The late "Father Pieps" of Concordia Seminary, St. Louis, taught me and many the meaning of evangelical catholicity, and of Lutheranism as a movement of gospel reform within and for the one church of Jesus Christ. To him I owe my devotion to an ecumenism that seeks to heal the breach of the 16th century in restored communion between Rome and the Reformation. I first met Pannenberg in the mid-'60s and have cherished our friendship ever since, not least because I consider his to be the most impressively ambitious theological project of our time. To him I owe my understanding of theology as the science of meaning in conversation and contestation with alternative constructions of reality. I hesitate to name just these two, for there are so many from whom I have learned and am learning, but in the constellation of my theological thought these two are, among contemporaries, the stars most firmly fixed.

In the intellectual culture, and especially in literary criticism, "postmodernism" has become a tired buzzword. However, my association with George Lindbeck in particular has persuaded me that the postmodern project in theology is filled with high promise. In *The Catholic Moment* I suggest some ways in which that project might be developed. Sustained conversation with the many theologians and other thinkers at our institute has brought me to an ever-deepening conviction that the Enlightenment's autonomous "way of the mind," aimed at achieving a cognitive and moral Esperanto of universal discourse, is utterly wrongheaded. This conviction has everything to do also with my understanding of the pluralism of culture and politics.

In discussing the constants and changes of one's mind, a word on how one thinks about one's vocation is in order. Here I must confess to a certain awkwardness. A constant is that I still believe the single most important work in the world is the proclamation of the gospel, the administration of the sacraments and the care of souls. One can receive no promotion from parish ministry. A change is that this is no longer my chief work. The awkwardness arises in that I want to persuade others that addressing the questions of religion and public life is not, as many seem to think, the most important work in the world. If it is not, I am asked, then why am I doing it? Because, as best as I can discern the matter, this is my vocation. It has taken me an embarrassingly long time to make my peace with the apparent truth that God wants me to do something less than the most important work in the world. And even now that peace is not secure.

These, then, are some of the continuities and discontinuities on a journey to the far side of the dark wood. I have painted in broad strokes. Every sentence calls for an article and every paragraph for a book. So I am dissatisfied with this account, but only for the moment. I have other opportunities to elaborate, amend and, when necessary, retract. We have all the time there is. Whether I am in the middle of life's journey or near its end really does not matter. If the former, I have arguments and projects in mind sufficient for at least a century. If the latter, the truth that has held the pieces together thus far convinces me that all will be well. The way ahead is bright with the knowledge that I need not know, and daily I begin to learn, as if for the first time, the wisdom of T. S. Eliot's assurance in *East Coker:* "For us, there is only the trying. The rest is not our business."

POSTSCRIPT: The above article was written in the early fall of 1989. A year later, on September 8, 1990, I was received into full communion with the Roman Catholic Church. I was very much pondering that step when this article was written. While the decision had by no means been made, the intimations of it are, I believe, evident in the article. I wrote that I expected to have "other opportunities to elaborate, amend and, when necessary, retract." My becoming a Catholic is an elaboration and amendment of what I wrote then. It is in no way a retraction. I am a Roman Catholic because I am the Lutheran who wrote this article. Why that should be is also something that I will, God willing, have opportunity to elaborate in the future.

Richard A. McCormick

Changing My Mind about the Changeable Church

C hange (implying a *terminus ad quem*) is intelligible only if we know the *terminus a quo* (the starting point). For me as an American Catholic theologian, that *terminus a quo* was the immigrant Catholic Church, the kind of church nostalgically memorialized in some of Andrew Greeley's novels. I was raised in that church, and some of my deepest religious and theological sensitivities — perhaps especially those I do not thematically recognize — took shape within it. Eugene Kennedy has described this church as follows:

> The unlettered Catholic who came to the United States in the last century fashioned a way of life within the host Protestant culture that was tight, intellectually narrow, and wrapped in an invisible and largely impermeable membrane that resisted social osmosis with the rest of the country. It was also the most successful era of development in the history of the Roman Catholic Church. This Catholic structure defended itself proudly against doctrinal and moral compromise; it was, above

---

Richard A. McCormick, S.J., is John A. O'Brien Professor of Christian Ethics at the University of Notre Dame, Notre Dame, Indiana.

all, obedient to the authority which was exercised for generations without any serious challenge by its bishops and clergy
and other religious teachers. Immigrant Catholicism was, in
fact, held together by the vigorous churchmen who retained
their power over their flocks by exercising it regularly on an
infinitely detailed category of behaviors, ranging from what the
faithful could eat on Fridays to what they could think or do in
the innermost chambers of their personal lives ["The End of
the Immigrant Church," *Illinois Issues*, August 1982, pp. 15-21].

The moral theology that I was taught and that for some
years I myself taught reflected the immigrant Catholic community Kennedy described as well as the ecclesiology that nourished
it. It was all too often one-sidedly confession oriented, magisterium dominated, canon law related, sin centered and seminary
controlled.

This represents my *terminus a quo*. In ten general areas
my mind has since changed or my perspective has shifted.
Interestingly, nearly all these changes pertain to ecclesiology;
but they have very significant impacts on moral theology, both
its method and its ultimate conclusions. Some of these perspective changes overlap significantly. That is not surprising
since all of them, in one way or another, trace back to Vatican II
and its ecclesiology. That council shook up the Catholic
Church in much the same radical and vigorous way that the
stirrings of freedom and democracy rocked the Eastern bloc
countries last year. It was bound to affect the way I viewed
myself, the church, the world and God, and therefore the way
I did theology.

The first area about which I've changed my mind is the
nature of the church. It is easy to fall into caricature here, and
I repent for that in advance. Still, I believe that my early view
of the church was dominantly pyramidal, with authority and
truth descending from above (pope and bishops) to rank-and-
file believers (the rest of us). This model powerfully supports
an ecclesiastical gnosticism that exempts the hierarchy from
standard forms of scholarly accountability and reduces the

theological task to mediating authoritative documents. This ul-tramontanism peaked during the reign of Pius XII. At that time few of us felt terribly threatened by the highly authoritarian and obediential motifs of *Humani generis.* That is, we thought, just the way things are. Many Catholics experienced little or no discomfort with the pyramidal model of the church. It seemed natural to them, indeed *juris divini.* In those days triumphalism was not a reproach.

All of this came tumbling down with Vatican II. The theo-logical and pastoral winds that blew freely from 1962 to 1965 led to a notion of church much more concentric than py-ramidal. My colleague Richard McBrien, in a talk to moral theologians at Notre Dame in June 1988, neatly summarized in six points Vatican II's major ecclesiological themes.

The first theme he emphasized is the church as mystery or sacrament. The church is a sign as well as an instrument of salvation. As a sacrament, it causes by signifying. As McBrien noted, this powerfully suggests the need to be attentive to justice issues within as well as outside the church. This prin-ciple of sacramentality undergirds the statement in the U.S. Catholic bishops' pastoral letter *Economic Justice for All:* "All the moral principles that govern the just operation of any economic endeavor apply to the church and its agencies and institutions; indeed the church should be exemplary" (no. 347).

The second theme is the church as people of God. All the faithful (not just the hierarchy and specialists) constitute the church. This has immediate implications for the elaboration and development of moral doctrine, for consultative processes and for the free flow of ideas in the church.

Third, the church as servant. Besides preaching the word and celebrating the sacraments, the church's mission includes addressing human needs in the social, political and economic orders. This suggests that these orders are also ecclesiological problems and that moralists and ecclesiologists must cooperate closely. It also suggests that moral theology, following John

Courtney Murray, must continue to probe the relationship between civic unity and religious integrity.

Another theme is the church as collegial. The church is realized and expressed at the local level (parish/diocese/region/nation) as well as the universal. Understanding this helps raise and rephrase the question of the use and limits of authority in the moral sphere, and the meaning of subsidiarity and freedom in the application of moral principles and the formation of conscience.

Fifth, the church as ecumenical. Being the whole body of Christ, the church includes more than Roman Catholics. The obvious implication is that Catholic officials and theologians must consult and take account of the experience, reflection and wisdom resident in other Christian churches.

Finally, McBrien noted the ecclesiological nature of the church. The church is a tentative and unfinished reality. It is *in via*. *A fortiori*, the church's moral and ethical judgments are always *in via* and share the messy, unfinished and perfectible character of the church itself.

That such ecclesiological themes have deeply affected my own thinking and theological work should be self-evident. Indeed, the following nine points are explications of these basic ecclesiological shifts.

I've also changed my mind about the importance of lay witness. Before Vatican II, conscience formation by Catholics was one-sidedly paternalistic. The individual would approach a priest, usually in confession, expecting him to be prepared to give the answers. The person would detail the facts; the confessor would assess them with a *licet* or *non licet*. This reflected the neat, if artificial, division of the church into the teaching and learning church.

Vatican II shattered this easy compartmentalization. It insisted that "it is for God's people as a whole with the help of the Holy Spirit, and especially for pastors and theologians, to listen to the various voices of our day, discerning and interpreting them, and to evaluate them in the light of the divine word." It went on to issue a remarkable summons to laypeople.

> Let the layman not imagine that his pastors are always such experts that to every problem which arises, however complicated, they can readily give them a concrete solution, or even that such is their mission. Rather, enlightened by Christian wisdom and giving close attention to the teaching authority of the Church, let the layman take on his own distinctive role [*Gaudium et spes*].

I confess that in my early years as a theologian I thought it was my mission to have answers to the most complicated problems. Where else would people get answers? The notion that laypeople have a distinctive — and indispensable — role to play in discovering moral truth was hardly promoted by their designation as "the learning church." I have come to see and value lay experience and reflection and am richer for it.

I've also reconsidered the limitation of papal and episcopal teaching competence. Catholics accept the fact that Christ commissioned the church to teach authoritatively in his name. Even though the manner of executing this commission has varied throughout history, Catholics still hold that this duty falls in a special way on the pope and the bishops in union with the pope. The formula used since the Council of Trent to state the reach of this hierarchical competence is *de fide et moribus* (matters concerned with faith and morals). Thus Vatican II stated: "In matters of faith and morals, the bishops speak in the name of Christ and the faithful are to accept their teaching and adhere to it with a religious assent of soul." The vague and sprawling nature of the phrase "faith and morals" fosters the idea that pope and bishops are equally and univocally competent on matters concerned with faith and morals.This would be particularly the case in a church conceived in a highly centralized and authoritarian way. In the encyclical *Magnificate Dominum*, Pius XII asserted that the power of the church over the natural law covered "its foundation, its interpretation, its application."

It is somewhat difficult to say exactly how my mind has changed here because I think that thought on this topic is still developing. Some years ago Karl Rahner argued that contemporary official formulations of the church's ordinary teaching competence are unnuanced. Furthermore, the American bishops in their pastoral letters on peace and the economy have distinguished between principles and their applications, and stated that the latter are "not binding in conscience." That is an old-fashioned way of saying that episcopal competence is not the same when the bishops are dealing with applications as it is when they propose general principles. This is significant when we remember that most of the controversial moral questions (for example, contraception) are matters of application of more general principles.

Just how we should state this hierarchical competence is not altogether clear. Undoubtedly, Pius XII had an overexpansive notion of his competence, built on the neoscholastic ecclesiology of his time. I do not suggest that pastors of the church should not offer moral judgments on human activities. Rather, I mean that the pope and bishops simply must consult those who are truly competent. Authority is not competence. Also, even after such consultation they must show appropriate caution and modesty. Horizontal activity in this world does not belong to the church's competence in the same way the deposit of faith does. Only with the ecclesiological moves made by Vatican II was I prepared to see this. Furthermore, I believe that a significant number of Roman curialists still do not share this view.

I have also reexamined ecumenism's role in the search for moral truth. Prior to Vatican II, serious ecumenism was in the quite lonely hands of a small band of theological pioneers. Official attitudes and practices were structured by the conviction that non-Catholic Christians were the adversaries of our central religious and moral tenets. Canon 1399,4 symbolized this. It forbade the reading of books written by Protestants that expressly treated religious themes. The very separation of non-

Catholics from the one true church constituted disparagement of their religious and moral thought. My preconciliar attitude toward the work of my non-Catholic peers was condescending tolerance, a civil nod that said, "Yes, but we have the last word."

Vatican II changed all that. Not only did it recognize the ecclesial reality of other Christian churches, but it stated explicitly that "whatever is wrought by the grace of the Holy Spirit in the hearts of our separated brethren can contribute to our own edification." Many of us in the field of moral theology learn more from our non-Catholic colleagues than we do from some Catholic theologians. The perspectives of the '40s and '50s that shaped many of us strike us now as incredibly defensive and parochial. At that time to think of the Lambeth Conference as a possible source of enlightenment appeared theologically ridiculous. Now it seems to be required.

My thoughts on the place of dissent have changed. In preconciliar decades, public disagreement with authoritatively proposed moral conclusions was virtually unheard of and would have been hugely dangerous for theologians. Yves Congar, O.P., has noted that the ordinary magisterium reached a kind of high watermark of one-sidedness in the pontificate of Pius XII. In *Humani generis* the pope stated two points. First, the ordinary magisterium of the pope requires total obedience. "He who listens to you listens to me." Second, the role — or *a* role — of theologians is to justify the declarations of the magisterium. The pope went so far as to say that once he had expressed his judgment on a point previously controversial, "there can no longer be any question of free discussion among theologians." In that atmosphere a dissenting theologian was doomed.

At the practical level what changed many of us — certainly me — was the 1968 encyclical *Humanae vitae* on birth regulation. I suspect it is very difficult for non-Catholics to appreciate the profound effect this had on Catholic theologians. For decades before that, theologians wrote and taught that artificial contraception was a serious moral wrong threatening spiritual health and ultimately salvation. Some even argued that the matter was infallibly taught in Pius XI's *Casti connubii.* The issue began to come unstuck in the mid-'60s when the so-called Birth Control Commission's majority argued that the traditional teaching could and should be modified. Then came *Humanae vitae,* reasserting the intrinsic moral evil of contraceptive acts. Most theologians viewed the reasoning as obviously flawed and indeed as discontinuous with major emphases in Vatican II. Their integrity demanded that they say so. They did.

Perhaps more important than the issue of birth regulation are the implications of this massive dissent. It suggested that the magisterium could be inaccurate even on an important moral question. It meant that "the light of the Holy Spirit, which is given in a particular way to the pastors of the church," as *Humanae vitae* describes it, does not guarantee lack of error or replace human analysis. It meant that the pope can choose the wrong advisers. It meant that a preoccupation with authority can itself lead to false steps. It meant that the church must be willing to examine its past formulations openly and critically, for there can be deficiencies "even in the formulation of doctrine," as Vatican II put it. It meant that honest theological input is called for both before *and after* official statements. All this indicates, of course, that respectful dissent should be viewed not as a disloyal challenge to authority but as a necessary valuable component of our growth in understanding. The *Humanae vitae* debate opened my eyes to my critical responsibilities as a theologian. I am comfortable with this even though the present policies of the Holy See are attempting — misguidedly, I believe — to dismantle the theological foundations of this comfort.

Therefore, I am no longer as certain of what is changeable and unchangeable in the church. The Catholic Church has endured for two millennia (notwithstanding some quite gaping holes in the bark of Peter). Catholics believe that it will, because of God's provident presence to it, endure to the end of time. It is easy to promote the idea that because the church will endure, so ought everything in and about it. This is particularly true in a community that sees itself uniquely commissioned to guard the deposit of faith, even to the point of infallibly proclaiming it. Thus it happens that we come to regard as unchangeable what is actually changeable. In doing so we provide powerful theological and emotional supports for institutional inertia.

One of many examples of this is the official teaching on contraception. The pope's connecting this matter with abiding doctrinal truths is theologically unjustifiable — a point the Cologne Declaration of German theologians underscored. Another example is the ordination of women. Official appeals to "God's plan" and "the will of Christ" try to transform the changeable into the unchangeable. I confess that prior to Vatican II, I would have viewed the ordination of women as forever impossible. Not so now. I have come to see it as not only possible but desirable and inevitable. I can cite two influences as largely responsible for this move. The first is the theology of Karl Rahner, who showed so often and so convincingly that what we once viewed as unchangeable really is not. The second is the privilege of experiencing personally the ministry of women. This has dissolved emotional obstacles that were far more formidable than any theological analysis anyway.

I would conclude, then, that by changing my attitudes on several deeply ingrained matters (such as contraception and women's ordination), I have uncovered a remarkably unthreatening attitude toward the changeable and unchangeable in the church in general.

I feel less compelled to claim certainty for my or the church's teachings. The Catholic Church, especially in the hundred years prior to Vatican II, seemed to believe it could achieve clarity and certainty in most moral matters, and that at a very detailed level. The pronouncements of the Holy See both generated and reinforced this belief. I suppose that a church that sees itself commissioned to teach authoritatively on moral questions and that lays claim to a special guidance of the Holy Spirit in the process might find it uncomfortable (at least) to say "I don't know." When I look over the book-size notes I drew

71

up for my students — on justice, sexuality, cooperation, the sacraments, etc. — I blush at the extent to which I shared this discomfort.

Credit it to wisdom, age or laziness — or a dash of all three: my old compulsion to be certain has yielded to an un-embarrassed modesty about many details of human life. Unlike some of my cantankerous and crusading coreligionists on the right, I am now quite relaxed in admitting with Vatican II that "the church guards the heritage of God's Word and draws from it religious and moral principles, without always having at hand the solution to particular problems." But of course!

I now also perceive differently the nature of effective teaching in the church. The church will always need to express itself clearly as it guards and promotes its inheritance. But this does not exhaust the meaning of effective teaching. If I have heard the following sentence once, I have heard it a thousand times: "The teaching of the church is clear." Clear, yes. Effective? Persuasive? Compelling? Meaningful? Those are different questions, questions whose importance some church leaders minimize or even fail to recognize — as I did earlier in my theological life.

Viewed from the perspective of the taught (rather than from the authority of the teacher), teaching is much more a matter of having one's eyes opened to dimensions of reality previously opaque. It is a personal and liberating appropriation, not submission to an authority.

There are many ways of opening eyes other than throwing encyclicals at problems. Witness is surely one of them. For example, the Jesuit martyrs of El Salvador have educated us enormously in the faith. Perhaps that is why the church trea-sures its martyrs: it knows that they are irreplaceable teachers. They say things textbooks cannot say. In this respect John Paul II is most effective as a teacher through his symbolic acts and liturgies and least effective when he explicitly sets out to teach. Somewhat similarly, the Catholic Church will remain a muted prophet if the witness of its own internal life speaks louder than its words — for example, in the area of fairness and human rights.

I have become more convinced of the imperative of honesty. The distinguished exegete John L. McKenzie recently noted that the Catholic Church is never further from Christ-likeness and the gospel than when it exercises its magisterium. Because McKenzie has not always conquered dyspepsia, it is easy and convenient to write off such a blast as the pouting of a habitual malcontent. That would be a mistake.

McKenzie's immediate concern is what he regards (rightly, I believe) as the injustice of the procedures against Charles Curran. But the matter is much larger than that. It is a question of honesty in magisterial procedures. I do not believe it is the cynicism of advancing age that emboldens me to note this. I think it is genuine love of the church.

Why is it that Rome generally consults only those who already agree with it? Why does Rome appoint as bishops only those who have never publicly questioned *Humanae vitae,* the celibacy of priests and the ordination of women? Why does a bishop speak on the ordination of women only after retirement? Why are Vatican documents composed in secrecy? Why does the Holy See not at least review its formulations on certain questions that it knows were met with massive dissent and nonreception? The coercive atmosphere established by the Holy See in the past decade provokes such questions about the honesty, and ultimately the credibility, of the teaching office. In my earlier years I would have thought that love of the church requires benign silence on such issues. Now silence appears to me as betrayal.

Finally, I have a new appreciation of the dynamic nature of faith. Because God's great culminating intervention in Jesus must be passed from generation to generation, it is very tempting to identify faith with adherence to the creedal statements that aid such transmission. This is especially true in the West, where reflection on the faith was for centuries eagerly hosted by universities. The Reformation understandably deepened the emphasis on propositional orthodoxy and thus contributed significantly to a one-sided view of faith that has endured even into the present, and especially in the coercive atmosphere of the present.

Actually, faith is a response of the whole person. It is not something that one has once and for all — like a book on a shelf, a pearl in a drawer, a diploma on a wall or a license in a wallet. It is not merely a practice, a statement or a structure. It is mysteriously both God's gift and our responsibility. We must recover and nourish it daily, in spite of our personal sins and stupidities, and in the face of the world's arrogant self-sufficiency. This task is much more daunting and frightening than propositional purity. It is the continuing personal appropriation of God's self-communication.

I find it ironic that the most radical change of my mind over the years has been a keener grasp of its own inadequacy when dealing with ultimacy.

Elisabeth Schüssler Fiorenza

Changing the Paradigms

The invitation to write about "how my mind has changed" is at once challenging and troubling. It challenges one to construct a narrative that can capture change that has not only private but also public significance. Yet a woman writer lacks narrative models for recording the public significance of her thought and work. This lack is doubly troubling for the woman writer who is a feminist, because feminism as a movement for transforming patriarchal structures and relations of domination understands change in a quite different way from that of the individualistic biographic tradition presupposed by the question of how one's "mind has changed."

The feminist theologian approaching this question faces an additional dilemma insofar as the religious narrative of the Western introspective confessional tradition grounds identity in culturally "feminine" terms. Women's spiritual autobiography, as Carolyn Heilbrun has observed, does not admit claims to achievement, independence and autonomy or allow for the recognition of one's accomplishments as due to something other than luck or grace. Biographies of outstanding women

---

Elisabeth Schüssler Fiorenza is Stendahl Professor of Divinity at Harvard Divinity School in Cambridge, Massachusetts.

conforming to the traditional narrative of womanliness or to the spiritual narrative of service cannot tell the stories of women's achievements as paradigmatic but only as exceptions to the rule, made possible by mere chance, inscrutable destiny or divine grace. Therefore, as Heilbrun argues in *Writing a Woman's Life*, we must reclaim for women an "impulse to power as opposed to the erotic impulse which alone is supposed to impel women. We know, we are without a text and must discover one." She insists, "women need to learn how publicly to declare their right to public power. . . . Power is the ability to take one's place in whatever discourse is essential to action and the right to have one's part matter."

If a woman who is a feminist theologian is to enter into the public introspective discourse shaping the story of important men in such a way that her insights matter, this discourse must change. This is especially true for public theological discourse, from which Christian women were excluded by law and custom for centuries. How is it possible to alter the discourse centering on male theological authorities in such a fashion that women's intellectual participation in it can matter? The search and struggle for recovering the theological voice of women by changing the discursive frameworks of theology in general and biblical studies in particular has absorbed my own thought and work in the past decade. Yet, as Nancy Miller has observed in a different context, women's quest for our own voices, stories and intellectual powers, for the ability to construct the world and the self in a different way, is fraught with danger. It is vulnerable because it lacks "plausibility" in a culture that defines women's identity and story in terms of love and attraction rather than power, thought and accomplishment.

I wanted to become many things when I was young: a hairdresser like my friend Rita, a poet like Goethe, an architect, a missionary and even a pope. Yet just as in the 1950s I could not imagine typing this article on a word processor, so could I not conceive of a woman as a theological scholar and authority in her own right. Although I fought for and achieved admission as the first woman to take the full program of theological studies that was reserved for priesthood candidates, I could not imagine as my male colleagues did that I could become a theologian like Karl Rahner, Rudolf Bultmann or Rudolf Schnackenburg — decisively determining theological questions and exegetical discussions. Every time a student comes up to me and asks with whom I studied feminist theology or a younger colleague says she was inspired to become a theologian or biblical scholar after hearing me lecture years ago, I realize how much the situation has changed.

If I were to divide my theological career into periods in terms of "how my mind has changed," these periods would roughly correspond to the past three decades. Although at the time I neither could conceive of myself as a theologian nor was I aware of the intellectual history of women's emancipation, the roots of my feminist theological work nevertheless go back to the 1960s. Recently a request for biographical information led me to look again at my first book on the practice and theology of women's ministries in the church, *Der vergessene Partner (The Forgotten Partner)*, published in 1964. I recalled that the last time I looked at the book, more than ten years ago, I felt embarrassed by the naïveté and piety of the young writer who sought to authorize her insights and proposals by quoting numerous theological, psychological and sociological authorities. This time around I had a different reaction. I marveled at the chutzpah of the young theological student who set out to write a thesis showing that the progressive theology articulated by such giants as Rahner or Yves Congar was inadequate, for it did not do justice to the pastoral praxis of women in the German Roman Catholic Church and in other Christian churches.

According to the publisher, some bishops considered the book too radical because it suggested that women should be involved in the spiritual formation of future priests. Moreover, I argued on theological grounds that women should demand ordination as bishops rather than just as deacons and priests. After this book was published I wrote an exegetical dissertation on priesthood in the New Testament which challenged me to rethink this proposal theologically. I argued (in a paper prepared in the late '60s for a conference held by St. Joan's Alliance) that women's incorporation into hierarchical-patriarchal structures can only lead to further clericalizing of the church — not to changing it. Since the sponsoring group advocated the ordination of women even to the lowest ranks of the patriarchal hierarchy, it refused to publish the paper.

Although my first book did not question hierarchical structures and theoretical frameworks, it had important methodological implications that I could not have articulated at the time. Anticipating feminist and liberation theologies, it assumed that the experience of women and the praxis of church and ministry should be primary for articulating ecclesiology and spirituality. Most important, though lacking theoretical self-consciousness, I nevertheless acted as a theological subject attempting to rethink theological constructions from the marginal location of a "lay" woman engaged in the study of theology. I became painfully aware of this marginalization when I applied for one of the two doctoral scholarships available for New Testament students. Although I had completed two advanced theological degrees summa cum laude and published a book, my *Doktor-vater* refused to obtain a scholarship for me, explaining that he did not want to waste the opportunity on a student who as a woman had no future in the academy.

The decade of the '70s was marked by my move to the U.S., the establishment of my teaching career, my experience of ecumenical collaboration and especially my encounter with the women's liberation movement in society, academy and church. Moving to the U.S., I abandoned my goal to integrate my training in New Testament exegesis with my interest in practical theology in a professional teaching career because the religious situation and ecclesial contexts in the U.S. are quite different from those in Germany. Instead I focused on New Testament scholarship, specializing in the interpretation of the Apocalypse. This was a fortuitous change of mind because practical or applied theology is still deemed less scholarly and the field of religious education still regarded as a woman's domain.

I was fortunate to begin my teaching career with a full-time graduate level position after completing my dissertation in Germany. Writing my first book and absorbing the emerging feminist literature to prepare for its translation into English had sensitized me to academic discrimination, especially against married women. Many institutions still had a written or un-written nepotism rule that prevented the employment of couples. They also maintained policies that restricted married women to part-time positions. Therefore, I insisted that I would come to the U.S. only if I could obtain a full-time graduate level appointment. When I attended my first meeting of the Amer-ican Academy of Religion/Society of Biblical Literature in 1971, I saw how unusual such an appointment was. This meeting brought together women members of academic societies in religion to initiate the Women's Caucus: Religious Studies. At this meeting I realized that most of the other married women present did not have full-time positions, even though in the '60s many departments were searching for qualified faculty.

It was most fortunate that I came to this country at a point when the women's movement in religion and the first attempts at articulating feminist theology began to emerge. Together with Carol Christ I became the first co-chair of the Women's Caucus: Religious Studies, which allowed me to get in touch with the ecumenical and intellectual development of this movement. Only later did I become involved with Roman Catholic groups such as the Women's Ordination Conference or the National Assembly of Religious Women, which contacted me because of my position at Notre Dame. Especially important was a sabbati-cal year at Union Theological Seminary (1974-75) when I par-ticipated regularly in the discussions of the New York Feminist Scholars in Religion launched by Carol Christ.

Together with my immersion in an interdenominational and interreligious academic dialogue, this ecumenical feminist discourse was extremely significant for the articulation of my own feminist theological perspective. It allowed me to move away from a certain theological parochialism characteristic of German theology departments and American Catholic universities. To elaborate a feminist theological analysis with women who brought to this discourse quite different religious experiences and institutional analyses proved crucial for articulating the theological paradigm shift in which we were engaged. The roots of the *Journal for Feminist Studies in Religion* which Judith Plaskow and I cofounded ten years later go back to this time.

Yet because of my previous research focus on women in the church and my acquaintance with political theology and critical theory (Francis Schüssler Fiorenza was a student of J. B. Metz and edited an issue of *Continuum* on Jürgen Habermas during the late '60s), I felt uneasy about two trends within the emerging feminist theological discourse. The first, an anti-intellectual posture, tended to foster gender-typing and assertions of feminine essentialism and did not allow for critical discussion and intellectual differences. Scholarship, research, academic theology, differentiated language, intellectual leadership and disciplined study were termed "male" and therefore rejected. Even today, feminist students will occasionally accuse me of "male scholarship" because my book *In Memory of Her* is full of footnotes and written in a "logical-linear" style. Although I can understand such a sentiment, given the bad experiences women have had in academic institutions, I could never share this view. It tends to replicate the cultural stereotype that restricts logical thinking and disciplined intellectual work to men and thereby prohibits women from producing knowledge and from defining the world.

A second worrying trend was that feminist theory, though it criticized binary oppositions and asymmetric dualisms, nevertheless tended to sustain such dualisms by conceptualizing patriarchy in terms of gender antagonism and male-female oppression rather than in terms of the complex interstructuring of sexism, racism, class-exploitation and colonialism in women's lives. Since many feminists accepted the premise that biblical religion forms the bedrock of Western patriarchy, feminist studies in religion developed a dualistic strategy with respect to organized religion. Feminist theology was typed as either reformist or revolutionary. This "either-or" option was often expressed theologically with the biblical symbol of "Exodus." Plaskow reflected on this split at the first national Jewish Women's Conference in 1973, delivering a paper titled "The Jewish Feminist: Conflict in Identities." In it she "explored both the sexism of the Jewish tradition" and the contradictions she felt at the time "between Judaism and feminism as alternative communities."

Although I fully shared the trenchant feminist critique of the Christian tradition, I never felt such an irreconcilable contradiction between my Christian and my feminist identity. In my experience some Christian teachings had offered a religious resource for resisting the demands of cultural feminine roles. Moreover, I grew up with the notion that all the baptized are the church and are responsible for its praxis. This ecclesial self-understanding had been theoretically validated during my doctoral studies. At the end of my sabbatical at Union I wrote two articles. One attempted to articulate my own feminist theological perspective as a "critical theology of liberation." The other used insights from the emerging scholarship on the social world of early Christianity to delineate the role of women in the early Christian movement. Both articles contained in embryonic form the major epistemological and theological issues that occupied my thinking in the 1980s. Together with my response at the first Women's Ordination Conference in 1975 they also caused professional-political difficulties after my return as a tenured professor from my sabbatical at Union.

In the past decade, most decisive for me has been not so much a change of mind as a change of academic-geographical location. When I accepted the invitation to join the faculty of the Episcopal Divinity School in Cambridge I had two compelling reasons: Aware of the Vatican's repression and removal of creative theologians in West German universities, I anticipated a similar development in the U.S. I made therefore a conscious decision not to remain in an academic situation where I would have to spend the rest of my career fighting ecclesiastical backlash. More important, EDS would allow me not only to develop my feminist theological interests in the context of the Boston Theological Institute and its rich theological and feminist resources, but also to focus on the theological education of women, since it provided the opportunity of developing a D.Min. program in feminist liberation theology and ministry. My move to Harvard Divinity School enhanced these opportunities. My theoretical explorations must be seen, however, not only in this context of theological education, but also in the context of my increasing involvement in feminist theological dialogue on a national and international level through lectures and workshops.

In the face of a growing religious right-wing backlash against civil rights movements, reactionary Christians and radical feminists alike have advocated a choice: either accept Christian teaching or become liberated and leave the bondage of patriarchal religion behind. This either-or position had political implications insofar as it neglected organized religion as a site for liberation struggles. It raised for me pressing theological questions: How could women reclaim the authority and resources of religion in the struggle to end patriarchal relations of subordination and exploitation? How could we cease to collaborate with our own religious oppression and at the same time claim our Christian birthright? How could we become religious agents and theological subjects in a patriarchal institution built on the silence and denial of women? How could we claim our theological voice and ritual power without being co-opted into becoming honorary churchmen? How could we articulate a *different* theology and praxis without becoming sectarian?

In order to address these questions I advocated the theological notion of "partial identification" and "spiritual resistance" at the Second Roman Catholic Women's Ordination

Conference in 1978. At the same time I was searching for a positive alternative to the Exodus image that could articulate a Christian feminist identity. The biblical symbol of Exodus with its historical roots in American feminism has great currency among feminists in biblical religions. It was dramatized by Mary Daly, theologized by Rosemary Radford Ruether and advocated by liberation theology. Nonetheless, this image tends to engender the illusion that women can move out of the bondage of patriarchy into a "promised land" or feminist "other world." Yet no space exists — not even in our own minds — that is a "liberated zone" to which we could move. Whereas some privileged women could move out of patriarchal institutions, most of us could not.

Rather than engage in the illusion of Exodus, feminist theology had to find a symbol that encouraged women in biblical religions to choose how and where to attack the many-headed dragon of patriarchy. Those of us who are privileged in terms of race, class and education, I argued, have to do so in solidarity with those women who must struggle daily against multiple forms of patriarchal oppression and dehumanization in order to survive. Not Exodus but struggle is the common ground for women.

To choose organized religion as a site of struggle for liberation presupposes a sense of ecclesial ownership as well as repentance of complicity with patriarchal religion. Such a feminist strategy needs to abandon both the dualistic conceptualization of women as mere victims of patriarchal religion *and* the submissive collaboration of women in patriarchal religion and church. Only when women understand ourselves *as* church and not just as passive bystanders in the church can we reclaim the church as the *ekklesia of women.*

Ekklesia, the Greek word for church, describes the democratic assembly of full citizens responsible for the welfare of the city-state. To link ekklesia or church with *women* makes explicit that women are church and always have been church. It asserts that women have shaped biblical religion and have the

83

authority to do so. It insists on the understanding and vision of church as the discipleship of equals. Thus women-church is not to be understood in exclusive, sectarian terms. Rather, it is a hermeneutical feminist perspective and linguistic consciousness-raising tool that seeks to define theologically what church is all about. As a movement it claims the center of biblical religion and refuses to relinquish its inheritance. Such an attempt to displace the feminist theological Exodus alternative requires a concept of patriarchy that can take into account women's different social locations.

Women of color have always insisted that white feminist theory must relinquish its dualistic conceptualization of patriarchy as the supremacy of all men and the equal victimization of all women and develop a feminist analysis that could uncover the interstructuring of sexism, racism, colonialism and class-exploitation in women's lives. They pointed to the invisibility of doubly oppressed women in the dualistic framework of feminist Euro-American theology. The appearance of Susan Moller Okin's study of Western political philosophy, *Women in Political Thought,* helped me to address theoretically this challenge of "Third World" women by developing a feminist systemic analysis that can distinguish between androcentric dualism and patriarchy. Patriarchy as a sociopolitical graduated male pyramid of systemic dominations and subordinations found its classical articulation in Aristotelian philosophy, which restricts full citizenship to Greek propertied, freeborn, male heads of households. The order of the patriarchal household becomes the model for the order of the state. It excludes freeborn women, slaves and barbarians — women and men — from citizenship and public leadership because their "natures" do not make them fit to "rule."

Patriarchy, which in its various mutations has persisted in antiquity and throughout recorded history, I argue, did not originate with Christianity but has been mediated by it. Although patriarchy as a complete sociopolitical system has been modified in the course of history, the classical politics of patriarchal domination has decisively shaped — and still does so today — modern Euro-American forms of democracy. At the heart of Western society resides the contradiction between patriarchal structures and democratic aspirations. This contradiction has produced ideological justifications for the political and intellectual exclusion of all but elite propertied men.

Modern civil rights and liberation movements thus can be understood as struggles against patriarchal deformations of democracy. The feminist movement in society and biblical religion prevails at the center of these struggles. Such a political reconceptualization of patriarchy allows one to distinguish between patriarchy and gender dualism, patriarchy and sexism. It helps one to conceptualize women's struggles for "civil rights" in the church and for our theological authority to shape Christian faith and community as an important part of women's liberation struggles around the globe.

This political reconceptualization of patriarchy and women's struggle had three important implications for my work as a biblical scholar. It allowed me to reconceptualize the study of "women in the Bible," by moving from what men have said about women to a feminist historical reconstruction of early Christian origins as well as by articulating a feminist critical process for reading and evaluating androcentric biblical texts. Such a critical feminist reconceptualization challenges the androcentric frameworks of the discipline as a whole.

First: The historical-political analysis of patriarchy and the struggles for democracy provided a reconstructive model that could make the agency and struggles of women historically visible. *In Memory of Her* does not seek to recover a feminist "golden age" in the beginnings of Christianity. Rather, it attempts to trace and make historically visible the visions and struggles of early Christian women and men in a patriarchal world. It seeks to reconstruct the points of tension between Christian vision and community and the patriarchal Greco-Roman society. It seeks to unmask historically and theologically how and why both the discipleship of equals and the patriarchal

male pyramid of subordination have become constitutive of
Christian identity throughout the centuries. Such a feminist
reconstruction of Christian origins requires a disciplined historical imagination that can make women visible not only as
victims but also as agents.

Second: Insofar as the Bible encodes both the "democratic" vision of equality in the Spirit as well as the injunctions
to patriarchal submission as the "Word of God," its interpretation must begin with a *hermeneutics of suspicion* that can unravel
the patriarchal politics inscribed in the biblical text. Since the
Bible is written in androcentric, grammatically masculine language that can function as generic inclusive or as patriarchal
exclusive language, feminist interpretation must develop a *hermeneutics of critical evaluation for proclamation* that is able to
assess theologically whether scriptural texts function to inculcate patriarchal values, or whether they must be read against
their linguistic "androcentric grain" in order to set free their
liberating vision for today and for the future. Such a feminist
hermeneutics of liberation reconceptualizes the understanding
of Scripture as nourishing bread rather than as unchanging
sacred word engraved in stone.

Third: The development of a feminist reconstructive-
historical model as well as of a critical hermeneutics for liberation would not have been possible without the theoretical
contributions of feminist historians, literary critics and political
philosophers. Yet feminist scholarship, despite the increase of
feminist theory in all academic disciplines in the past decade,
continues to be marginalized under the heading "woman" as
peripheral to biblical and theological discourse. Therefore those
of us who sought to initiate a feminist theological paradigm
shift in the early 1970s must now concentrate on changing the
disciplinary discourses of academic religious scholarship and of
Christian theologies. In my SBL presidential address and in my
convocation address when beginning my tenure at Harvard
Divinity School, I argued that theological disciplines and institutions must explicitly reflect on their rhetorical, public,

sociopolitical functions. Only when religious and biblical studies decenter their stance of objectivist positivism and scientific value-detachment and become "engaged" scholarship can feminist and other liberation theologies participate in defining the center of the discipline. Not the posture of value-detachment and apolitical objectivism but the articulation of one's social location, interpretive strategies and theoretical frameworks are appropriate in such a rhetorical paradigm of theological studies. In the course of graduate theological education students need to acquire not only methodological but also hermeneutical sophistication fitting to such a rhetorical paradigm.

Whereas in the '70s my "public image" was marked by scholarly bifurcation — among scholars I was known as an "expert" on the Apocalypse and among women as an emerging feminist theologian — this perception has changed dramatically in the '80s. While some regret the "ideological deviation" tarnishing my scholarly reputation, many take pride in and draw courage from my theological work. As Dorothy L. Sayers puts it: "Time and trouble will tame an advanced young woman, but an advanced old woman is uncontrollable by any earthly force." It is gratifying not to have been tamed.

David Tracy

God, Dialogue and Solidarity:
A Theologian's Refrain

To respond to the question "How has your mind changed (or remained the same) in the past ten years?" is initially disorienting. It seems to demand a degree of self-consciousness about one's work that may be undesirable. Most of us carry our continuities of desire, hope, beliefs, opinions and judgments more subconsciously than consciously as we move forward month by month, year by year. Readers and friends have proven this by helping me see more clearly where I've really "changed" in thought or sensibility than I would have realized on my own. Perhaps that is part of what Schleiermacher meant by his famous statement that good interpretation means "to understand the author better than the author understands himself." For once one has written a work, the work lives on its own. The author becomes another reader — with some privileged knowledge of what she or he once meant, but with no hermeneutical privilege at all in interpreting what

David Tracy is Andrew Thomas Greeley and Grace McNichols Greeley Distinguished Service Professor of Catholic Studies at the Divinity School of the University of Chicago.

the text actually says. For that latter task, for better and for worse, the work alone speaks.

Like most disorienting questions, however, this one can help theologians to reorient, or at least to see what has been the general direction of their work and what significant differences, detours and interruptions have occurred. The fine theologian Jean-Pierre Jossua once told me that he rereads Proust every ten years in order to find out what has happened to himself. It is a wise choice, for Proust's texts, so meditative, slow in pace, self-reflective and demanding in concentration, are unequaled in their power to make one reflect on both "time lost" and "time regained." These last few months I have been rereading Tolstoy's later works and Simone Weil's for largely the same reasons. Jossua, I observe, did not reread his own work to try to understand his changes. Nor, I confess, have I reread my work. What I attempt here is to reflect on what, at this moment, seems to me reasonably clear about the continuities and shifts in my own attempts to pursue that almost impossible — but for me necessary — mode of inquiry, theological reflection.

First, the continuities. Like many others in our confusing theological period, I have spent a great deal of time (perhaps too much) on theological method. Here I continue to believe that some form of revised correlational method (i.e., correlating an interpretation of the tradition with an interpretation of our situation) remains the best hope for theology today. I have continued to revise my form of correlation method when it seemed necessary. For example, I have for the last ten years (but not before) always added the important qualifier "mutually critical" to the word "correlation" in order to indicate the fuller range of possible correlations between some interpretation of the situation and some interpretation of the tradition. This signals that theological correlation is not always harmonious (much less "liberal"), but covers the full range of logically possible relationships between situation and tradition from nonidentity (or confrontation) through analogy to identity. I have also tried to give more attention in several essays and one book *(Plurality and Ambiguity)* to the kind of public criteria necessary to adjudicate the inevitable clashes between the claims to meaning and truth in both situation and tradition. Hence my efforts over the last ten years to retrieve, rethink and indeed radically revise William James's suggestive criteria for "on-the-whole" judgments. I have elsewhere formulated, therefore, a threefold set of criteria: first, the hermeneutical concept of truth as primordially "manifestation"; second, cognitive criteria of coherence with what we otherwise know or, more likely, believe to be the case; third, ethical-political criteria on the personal and social consequences of our beliefs.

For some of us the demand for public criteria for all truth-claims remains both the initial impetus and the great hope for all contemporary theology, whether liberal or post-liberal, neoorthodox or neoconservative, modern or post-modern, reformist or revolutionary, contextualist or universalist. This remains the case insofar as Christian theologians mean what they say when they say "God" or any other universal ethical or cognitive demand that such God-language (theology) necessarily involves. True, we are all deeply embedded in particular contexts, and this contextual reality makes the warranting of universal claims exceedingly difficult. And surely God is universal, or we are speaking either nonsense or Zeus-talk, not Yahweh-talk. This complexity necessitates further attention to questions of criteria and method — not only, let us note, in theology but across all the modern disciplines where the inevitable strife over method shows no sign of abating.

In sum, I shall have to continue to work on theological method questions as the questions and dilemmas of developing theology in our pluralistic and ambiguous situation multiply (as they surely will). I have always been thankful that my major mentor in theology, Bernard Lonergan, devoted his entire painstakingly intellectual life to questions of method. I am also thankful that I have spent the last 20 years at the University of Chicago Divinity School, an institution noted (or infamous) for its concern for method in religious studies, history of religion, philosophy and theology. At the same time, I have come to acknowledge far more than I did ten years ago that Karl Rahner (no stranger to questions of theological method himself) was right when he stated, "But we cannot spend all our time sharpening the knife; at some point we must cut."

The only way to cut accurately is to try to analyze questions of method simultaneously with substantive theological topics. That was the strategy behind my book on fundamental theology *(Blessed Rage for Order)* and my book on systematic theology *(The Analogical Imagination)*. About half of each book is on method, the other on testing the method with substantive theological issues (God, revelation, Christ). If I can ever successfully think my way forward to the most complex task of all, practical theology, the same ratio will hold: the principal methodological issue will be the relationship of theory and praxis in both personal and social terms, and the principal theological topics will be Spirit and church. I may never be ready to attempt that third volume of the projected trilogy; I know that I am not ready now. I make that unhappy admission not just because I still do not know my own mind clearly and systematically enough about four central issues of that practical theology task — contemporary social theory, ethics, ecclesiology and the history of spirituality. It is also, indeed primarily, because I have changed the focus of my theological thought.

The hopes of modernity, including modern theology, are noble ones. I have shared in these hopes, especially in my book *Blessed Rage for Order,* and to a large extent I still do. One need only reread Kant's classic essay "What Is Enlightenment?" to understand — or better, to sense — what was and is at stake in the hopes of modernity. Better yet, one should read Andrei Sakharov and Václav Havel. In both society and church, the need to fight against obscurantism, mystification and outright oppression is as clear now as it was in the 18th century. The need to defend reason, often against its presumed guardians (e.g., positivism and scientism), remains clear to all not tricked into intellectual and moral languor by too-easy assaults on the modern heritage. On theological questions, the same truth obtains: for example, Protestant neoorthodoxy, as Wilhelm Pauck insisted, is a self-critical moment within the liberal tradition; it was not and should not become a return to a premodern orthodoxy. Even "postmodernity," that ever-elusive word in search of a definition, is more an acknowledgment that we now live in an age that cannot name itself than that we should simply reject modernity.

Nevertheless, there are good reasons to understand our period and our needs as more postmodern than modern. Part of the change is clearly cultural: we no longer assume the cultural superiority of Western modernity. Anyone who continues to think and write (as many in the modern Western academy still do) as if other cultures either do not exist or exist only as steppingstones to or pale copies of Western modernity is self-deluding. Most of us now find bizarre those 19th-century Whig historians like Macaulay with their sublime confidence that true history means what leads up to and finds its glorious culmination in us, the "moderns." A similar fate has overtaken modern liberal philosophical and theological schemas (such as those of Hegel, Schleiermacher, Troeltsch and Rahner) on the relationship of Christianity to the other religions.

Another aspect of the theological change from modernity to postmodernity is the new ecclesial situation. The Eurocentric character of Christian theology surely cannot survive in a Christianity that is finally and irreversibly becoming a world church. That there are now more Anglicans in Africa than in Great Britain, more Presbyterians in South Korea and Taiwan than in Scotland, and that there will probably be more Roman Catholics at the close of this century in the Southern Hemisphere than in the Northern should give us all pause. No modern theologian can continue to assume that European and North American modes of Christian thought and practice can, even in principle, any longer suffice for an emerging world church.

Another part of the question of postmodernity focuses less on cultural or ecclesial shifts than on more strictly intellectual problems. Without serious rethinking, the Enlightenment notion of rationality is in grave danger of becoming part of the problem, not the solution. That is even the case for those, like myself, who continue to believe that the very nature of the claims of theology demands public, indeed transcendental or metaphysical, explication. This mode of reflection (for Kant, Hegel, Schleiermacher; for Rahner, Tillich and Whitehead in their competing formulations) always was difficult. But it was also, with great effort, available (viz., by formulating classical metaphysics into modern transcendental terms). The acknowledgment of the role of language (and thereby history) in all understanding combined with the awareness of the large role unconscious factors play in all conscious rationality have made those theologically necessary transcendental forms of reflection not impossible, but far, far more difficult to formulate adequately than modern theology (including my own) once believed.

The modern notion of the self, like the modern notion of rationality, also needs radical rethinking — especially in new theological anthropologies. The theological language of sin and grace once spoke of a decentered ego with all the force of the most radical French postmodernists. Anyone who doubts this ought to reread that brilliant, genre-conscious postmodernist (not existentialist) Søren Kierkegaard on sin, grace and the decentered Christian self. Even the otherwise happy recovery of the traditions of Christian spirituality in our day are also in danger of becoming further fine-tuning, further new peak experiences for the omnivorously consuming modern self.

In sum, there is a dark underside to modern thought, including modern theology. Anyone who senses this problem at all is likely to attempt one or another form of postmodern theology. Some forms of this will prove straightforwardly anti-modern, as in the profound but disturbing reflections of Alexander Solzhenitsyn, the Augustinian pessimism pervading the theology and restorationist policies of Cardinal Josef Ratzinger or a good deal of the rhetoric (if, happily, not the practices) of some of the neo-Barthian theologies. Other forms will prove more clearly postmodern, such as Gustavo Gutiérrez's powerful reflections on contemporary theology's need to face the reality of the "nonperson" of the oppressed in the massive global suffering surrounding us, as distinct from modern theology's more typical concern with the "nonbeliever"; and the many alternative forms of postmodern theologies in feminist, womanist, African-American and global liberationist struggles and theologies. Still others will embrace postmodernity in its most decentering, deconstructive forms so fully that "a-theologies" will be born to announce, yet again, that the "death of God" has finally found its true hermeneutical home.

In the midst of all this, it is perhaps a little odd to say that my own theology has two principal foci: a hermeneutics in which the "other," not the "self," is the dominant focus; and a theological insistence that only a prophetic-mystical form of theology for naming God can help us now. Odd, but for me necessary.

I focus on hermeneutics because one way to respond to the crisis of modernity and the ambiguous arrival of postmodernity is to reflect anew on the problem of interpretation itself. In fact, the question of interpretation has always been a central issue in times of cultural crisis. So it was for Aristotle and the Greek Stoics in the waning days of the Greek classical age. So it was for the development of allegorical methods for interpreting classical religious texts by Stoic, Jewish and Christian thinkers in the Hellenistic period. So it became for Augustine in that watershed of late classical antiquity and the emerging medieval period. Again hermeneutics came to the center of attention with the explosive arrival of Martin Luther. In early modernity, moreover, from Descartes and Spinoza through Schleiermacher and Hegel, the problem of hermeneutics demanded attention from all those classic moderns concerned to learn new ways to interpret their classic texts in a now new, because modern, setting. The full-fledged arrival of historical consciousness in theology, best viewed in the often tortured, always honest, reflections of both Troeltsch and Lonergan, only heightened the need for new reflection in hermeneutics.

"May you live in interesting times," says an ancient Chinese curse. Unfortunately, our choice is not when to live, but only how. This is not a time when Western culture needs one last burst of overweening, indeed hubristic, self-confidence masking self-absorption and newfound insecurity. At this time we all need to face the strong claims on our attention made by other cultures and by the other, subjugated, forgotten and marginalized traditions in Western culture itself. We also need to face the ambiguous otherness within our own psyches and traditions. The last great attempt to salvage modernity — indeed, so great an attempt that it bears all the marks of classical Greek tragedy — was Husserl's *Crisis of the European Sciences*. After that, the deluge.

Amid the often conflicting strategies for rethinking our situation and thereby rethinking our pluralistic and ambiguous heritage, contemporary hermeneutics can prove of some aid. From the exposés of the illusions of modern conscious rationality by Freud, Marx and Nietzsche through contemporary feminist theory, modernity has been forced to rethink its Enlightenment heritage on both reason and the self in increasingly radical — that is, postmodern — de-centering forms. Central here has been postmodern rereadings of Freud, Marx and Nietzsche, especially by feminist thinkers. Or consider Walter Benjamin's willingness to rethink the classic traditions he so loved, now guided by the hermeneutical acknowledgment that "every great work of civilization is at the same time a work of barbarism." Consider Foucault's noble attempts to rethink and retrieve the "subjugated" knowledge of our own past. In every case of serious postmodern thought, radical hermeneutical rethinking recurs. Little wonder that the most marginalized groups of our heritage — mystics, hysterics, the mad, fools, apocalyptic groups, dissenters of all kinds, avant-garde artists — now gain the attention of many postmodern searchers for an alternative version of a usable past.

The emergence of a hermeneutical consciousness is clearly a part of this cultural shift. For hermeneutics lives or dies by

95

its ability to take history and language seriously, to give the other (whether person, event or text) our attention as other, not as a projection of our present fears, hopes and desires. The deceptively simple hermeneutical model of dialogue is one attempt to be faithful to this shift from modern self to postmodern other. For however often the word is bandied about, dialogue remains a rare phenomenon in anyone's experience. Dialogue demands the intellectual, moral and, at the limit, religious ability to struggle to hear another and to respond — to respond critically, and even suspiciously when necessary, but only in dialogical relationship to a real, not a projected, other.

My own attempts in the last ten years to enter into interreligious dialogues have revealed the same kind of hermeneutical need to attend to a real, not a projected, other. Consider the crucial need to rethink the Christian relationship to indigenous traditions (still often misnamed "pagan" or even "primitive") by facing the history of Christian projections upon and oppression of those traditions in Europe, Asia, Africa, Oceania and the Americas. Consider the needs of Jewish-Christian dialogue in a post-Holocaust situation. How can we pretend to take history with theological seriousness and then ignore the Holocaust? If we do ignore it, then we should either admit the bankruptcy of all theological talk of history as the locus of divine action and human responsibility or admit that we consider only the "good" parts of our history worthy of theological reflection.

With the Jew and the so-called pagan, the Christian in dialogue (which demands, in practice, solidarity) needs to face the constant Christian temptation to project a Christian consciousness upon the other. Both the "pagan" and the Jew have too often served as the projected other of "Christian" self-understanding. When in dialogue with the Buddhist, Christians need to face not a projected other but this great other tradition with its profound vision of ultimate reality as emptiness *(sunnyata)*. Buddhists speak and live that vision so persuasively that, in first meeting them, Christian theologians like myself are hurled into a state of such initial confusion that it bears all the marks of an experience of the *mysterium fascinans et tremendum.* Dialogue with Buddhists has forced me to rethink theologically the more radically apophatic mystics of the tradition, especially Meister Eckhart.

Dialogue with Buddhists has also forced me to see how even so classic a Christian witness as Francis of Assisi can be allowed to speak anew to all Christians concerned to establish new relationships to all creatures (not only humans) and thereby to the whole earth. This may seem a strange claim, for Francis of Assisi is the one Christian saint whom all Westerners profess to love, even if most quietly continue to view him as a kind of holy fool who somehow wandered off the pages of Dostoyevski. But the usual view of Francis is no longer even the noble one of Dostoyevski's holy fool; Francis now lives in common memory as something like the lost eighth member of Walt Disney's seven dwarfs, somewhere between Happy and Bashful. But Francis was in fact — as Buddhists see clearly — a Christian of such excess and challenge to ordinary, even good, Christian ways of understanding all of God's creation as beloved that we still cannot see him clearly. We have not yet, in Christian theological dialogue, taken even Francis of Assisi seriously.

Dialogue with the women mystics or the Shakers also would make one radically rethink one's own heritage. The hermeneutical turn in theology is a difficult and demanding practice just as it is a necessarily complex theory.

If we are to hear one another once again, then dialogue and solidarity amid the differences and conflicts that dialogue may demand is our best present hope. There is no escape from the insight that modernity most feared: there is no innocent tradition (including modernity), no innocent classic (including the Scriptures) and no innocent reading (including this one). My hope is in genuinely dialogical thought accompanied by real solidarity in action. Otherwise we are back where we began: with officially exorcised but practically dominant programs of Western and modern stories of progress; with monological forms of rationality and increasingly brittle notions of a self seemingly coherent but actually possessive and consumerist; with "others" present, if at all, only as projections of our modern selves, our desires, wants, needs.

My experience and conviction is also that sometimes the best road to hermeneutical retrievals of tradition is through critique and suspicion. One route to retrieval is facing the disturbing otherness within ourselves and our traditions as well as the reality of others waiting, no longer patiently, to speak. It is no small matter that now many "others" do theology in ways very different, even conflictually other, from my own white, male, middle-class and academic reflections on a hermeneutics of dialogue and a praxis of solidarity. They bespeak critiques, suspicions and retrievals of the Christian theological heritage that I too need to hear far better than I have to date. Uniting so many of these new voices, it seems, is not a theory of hermeneutics, much less a revised correlational method for theology, but a new hermeneutical practice that actualizes that theory and that method better than many of the theorists do.

This new hermeneutical practice become living theology is best described as "mystical-prophetic." The hyphen is what compels my interest. For these classic religious types are just as much figures of religious excess as of theological conflict. How can we think of such two different modes of religious otherness together? That is the question toward which much serious theology today strives. In *The Analogical Imagination* I tried to rethink the traditional Christian theological dialectic of sacrament and word as the more primordial religious dialectic of "manifestation" and "proclamation." I continue to believe that such a religious dialectic is at the heart of Christianity. But I now see more clearly — thanks to the voices of the new theologies allied with the welcome recovery of spirituality within theology — that in practice and thereby in theory this pervasive religious dialectic of manifestation and proclamation is best construed theologically as mystical-prophetic.

How, therefore, can we find anew the power to name God in a mystical-prophetic way? That is theology's central postmodern question. The theological center of gravity of all Christian theology is the God disclosed in Jesus the Christ. My own major concern, therefore, has been to try to rethink how Christian theology first came to name God. In a perhaps overambitious but necessary work in progress, I am trying to rethink how Christian theology, in fidelity to the Christian religion and the demands of critical reflection, first rendered its names for the God of Jesus Christ in dialectically mystical-prophetic ways. This effort demands new hermeneutical attention to the otherness of the forms disclosing the content in the narratives of the synoptic Gospels, the meditative narrative of John and the relentless dialectic of Paul. It also demands close attention to the otherness of the forms of dialogue in Plato, the treatise in Aristotle and tragedy among the classic Greeks. In the puzzling history of these often conflicting forms disclosing their contents through the form lies the secret, I have come to believe, of Christian theology, that puzzling hybrid of Jewish and Greek forms and contents. Through these forms we first learned to name God theologically.

How Christian theology — that always elusive, always reflectively necessary, form of naming God — first emerged could provide some central clues needed, even now, for how we might be able to hear God even as we attempt to listen to one another in the minefield of modernity, postmodernity and antimodernity. Is it possible to find a contemporary naming of God that renders God's reality in forms that unite excess with elegance, mysticism with both rigorous intellectuality and the ethical-political seriousness of the prophets?

Perhaps not. But this much is clear: to say and mean "God" is what must drive all theology, whenever, wherever and whoever speaks. Those who doubt this should join me, at this ten-year juncture, in rereading the later Tolstoy and Simone Weil. They knew, for they managed to render God's name with some of the originating power of the Gospel narratives. And they rendered that name in and through the honest confusions, terrors and hopes of this age, our age — the age that cannot name itself.

Peter L. Berger

Reflections of an
Ecclesiastical Expatriate

Every ten years, it seems, the editors of *The Christian Century* ask me to write a piece on how my mind has changed. At first I'm pleased: Those people in Chicago still remember me; what is more, they apparently think their readers would still be interested in my ideas. Then, after this first flush of self-indulgent gratification, the request takes on a slightly threatening quality. One disturbing thought obtrudes: Have I really developed my intellectual position in an interesting way during the past decade? For as long as I can remember, *The Christian Century* has been the principal forum for mainline Protestantism; yet that is a world completely foreign to me at this point, a world that, despite its continuing importance in my own society, barely attracts my attention and is nearly irrelevant to my ongoing concerns. This is a disturbing and puzzling observation. It stopped me short and forced me to reflect.

I encountered this world of the mainline almost immediately upon coming to America not long after World War II. I was young, very poor, European and Lutheran, and wartime

---

Peter L. Berger is University Professor at Boston University.

desperations had shaped my social and religious sensibilities. America constituted an immense liberation from all this, a deeply satisfying experience of normality. The Protestant world I met fully represented the same normality. It was thoroughly identified with American culture, sensible, tolerant, far removed from the Kierkegaardian extremism that had up to then defined Christianity for me. It is hardly surprising that I had difficulties coming to terms with it.

While I could not accept the religio-cultural amalgam of the mainline churches, I found an ecclesiastical home right away in what was then the United Lutheran Church in America. It met both my religious and social needs. To be sure, the ULCA at that time was very much an American institution, and as such it partook of American normality (which, much later as a sociologist, I would call the "OK world" of middle-class America). It was not a locale for desperate leaps of faith. However, it was sufficiently and clearly enough Lutheran to remain distinct from the pervasive *Kulturprotestantismus* of the other mainline churches. As one participated in its services enough "otherness" was present to assure one that what was being worshiped was not simply the goodness of the American way of life. While I was prepared to affirm the goodness of America, I was not prepared to worship it or to equate its morality with Christian faith. After all these years, it seems to me I was quite correct in making this distinction.

The ULCA has disappeared, as has most if not all that was distinct in its successor denominations. Recently a cult of denigration has replaced the celebration of America, and various fashionable fanaticisms (all of them political rather than religious) have reduced the easygoing tolerance of that earlier period. But, curiously, what has not changed at all is the underlying principle of every variety of culture-religion: that the churches should reflect the moral concerns of their social milieu; even more, that the faithfulness of this reflexivity is the criterion by which the legitimacy of the churches' role must be judged. This principle can survive, and in this case has survived, even radical changes in the culture. I continue to believe, as I did those many years ago, that this principle is false and that it violates the very core of Christian faith.

It is always easier to perceive differences than continuities. Indeed, at first glance the differences between mainline Protestantism in the 1950s and the 1980s appear dramatic. The appearance is not deceptive. John Murray Cuddihy has written eloquently on the "Protestant smile," the *certain sourire* of ingenuous niceness that he rightly saw as a sacrament of American civility. This smile still exists in many places, both inside and outside the mainline churches, but is much less evident on the public face of American Protestantism. That face now has a set and sour mien, an expression of permanent outrage. A Protestant scowl has replaced the Protestant smile. Feminism more than anything else has set this tone in recent years. This grimly humorless ideology has established itself as an unquestioned orthodoxy throughout the mainline churches. A newcomer to American Protestantism today would hardly be struck by an atmosphere of easygoing tolerance.

One of my first jobs after coming to this country was as an office boy in the headquarters of the Methodist Church, which was then on lower Fifth Avenue in Manhattan. I vividly recall walking down long corridors and looking through open doors into the offices: almost every office was occupied by a formidable-looking woman (I have been puzzled by the charge that American Protestantism was a patriarchate; what impressed me then was how very feminized it was). Almost every one of these women was smiling.

I didn't quite trust the Protestant smile, though I found it agreeable enough. I tried to understand it. Though my reasons for taking up sociology of religion in particular were somewhat more complicated, decoding the Protestant smile was one of my early preoccupations. The result of this intellectual effort was my first publication, *The Noise of Solemn Assemblies*. The book came out in 1961 and attracted a certain amount of attention at the time; I still think it was a fairly adequate piece of analysis.

What has happened since those days of smiling Protestantism has been an essentially simple process, one that holds no sociological mysteries. It has been the working-out of two sociologically well-known forces, those of class and of bureaucracy. I have written elsewhere at great length about this development, but a brief restatement is in order.

Mainline Protestantism has always been in a symbiotic relationship with the middle-class culture, which is to a large extent its own historical product (after all, it is this type of Protestantism that has been a crucially important factor in the formation of American bourgeois civilization) and that continues to be its social context. In the 1950s mainline Protestant churches reflected the middle-class culture and constituted a sort of social establishment within it. Put sociologically, the principal function of these churches was to legitimate the middle-class culture of America, to certify that the latter was indeed "OK." The omnipresence of the national flag in churches (which at first shocked me) was a fitting symbol of this legitimating function. Once again it should be stressed that nothing is intrinsically pejorative about this understanding of the American church-society relationship. To the extent that one approves of the traditional middle-class values (by and large, I did), one will not necessarily be offended by their being religiously legitimated.

The offense, if any, is theological rather than moral. One will be offended theologically if one believes that the Christian faith must never be identified with any culture, not even with a culture that one finds morally acceptable or even admirable. America, despite its many faults, has been a remarkable moral experiment in human history; but America is not and never can be the kingdom of God. In other words, the key issue here is the transcendence of Christian faith: the kingdom of God is not of this world, and any attempt to make it so undermines the very foundation of the gospel.

What has changed is *not* the symbiotic church-society relationship of mainline Protantism; rather, what has changed is the character of the society, more specifically of the middle-class society and culture that is the natural habitat of the Protestant churches. This change is, more or less accurately, formulated by the so-called New Class hypothesis. In America (and, incidentally, in all other advanced capitalist societies) the middle class has split. Whereas previously there was one (though internally stratified) middle class, there now are two middle classes (also internally stratified). There is the old middle class, the traditional bour- geoisie, centered in the business community and the old profes- sions. But there is also a new middle class, based on the production and distribution of symbolic knowledge, whose members are the increasingly large number of people occupied with education, the media of mass communication, therapy in all its forms, the advo- cacy and administration of well-being, social justice and personal lifestyles. Many of these people are on the public payroll, employed in all the bureaucracies of the modern welfare, redistributive and regulatory state; many others, while working in private-sector institutions, are heavily dependent on state subsidies. This new middle class, inevitably, has strong, vested interests; equally inevi- tably, it has developed its own subculture. In other words, as is the case with every rising class (Marx has taught this well), what is at work here is a combination of class interest and class culture.

The class interest, within the political spectrum of Western democracies, is on the left; in America this means "liberal," in current terminology. The reason for this is extraordinarily simple. This class has a vital interest in the maintenance and expansion of those state expenditures on which its social exis- tence depends. Put differently, its class interest is in government rather than in the market, in redistribution rather than in produc- tion of societal wealth. The old middle class, for equally simple reasons, has opposing interests. Therefore it tends toward the political right; in America, this constitutes a "conservative" ten- dency. These interests, of course, are rarely stated as such in public political rhetorics. Class interests are presented as general interests. Businesspeople continue to believe, *mutatis mutandis,* that "what is good for General Motors is good for America"; the new middle-class professionals, no doubt with equal sincer- ity, believe that the "reordering of national priorities" that guarantees their privileges benefits the poor, the underclass or whatever other morally acceptable beneficiary can be plausibly cited. Whether or not these respective class interests represent these more general social goods is an empirical question that has little to do with public legitimation.

Class interest and class culture are never related in a perfectly functional manner. There were good functional reasons why the rising bourgeoisie emphasized the virtues of frugality and literacy; it would be hard to detect a comparable functionality in the particular manners and canons of aesthetic taste that came to be associated with bourgeois culture. However, while there is a degree of randomness in the manner by which a class acquires its cultural accoutrements, once acquired the latter do fulfill an important function. Members of a class can now recognize each other — sniff each other out — by means of the institutionalized cultural signals. Clothes, table manners, speech and expressed opinions serve to identify individuals for purposes of inclusion and exclusion. Once more, this is particularly important for a rising class, which has not yet firmly established its societal footing. This goes for the corporate dining room as it does for the faculty club; in each case, the cultural signals are known and quite easily recognized. As the new middle class took on a visible shape in the '60s its cultural signals too became known and recognizable. This new middle class identified itself, logically enough, as *not* being the old middle-class culture. "Bourgeois" became a negative word. Logically again, the new middle-class culture understood itself as "emancipatory" or "liberating" as against the traditional bourgeois virtues. Strictly speaking, it was just that. The break was most visible in the areas of sexual and gender behavior, but it was by no means limited to these.

There was, however, one big difference between this and earlier rising classes. Much of the new middle class is actually in the business of culture, is in control of many of the institutions that produce and disseminate cultural symbols, notably in the educational system and the communication media. In consequence the new middle class has a cultural clout enormously larger than one might expect from its relatively modest numbers and financial resources (the latter are considerable, but still modest when compared to the economic might of the business community). This evaluation explains many of the political successes of the new middle class, whose values and views continue to represent a minority of the population. What is more, because of this control over the cultural apparatus, the new middle class has successfully infiltrated its "class enemy" with many of its own ideas, agendas and lifestyles. The business community, by contrast, is culturally passive and inept as it has always been. The "thinkers" are elsewhere. As to the working class, it has always been the weakest party in the drama of bourgeois cultural imperialism. It resists where it can by using its sheer numbers in the democratic process and by a sort of sullen sabotage of the agendas of its "betters," but it lacks the cultural know-how by which an effective resistance could be mounted. Thus there has been an inequality in the cultural battles of recent decades; the new middle class has generally been on the offensive. Of course, this does not mean that it always wins. Its agenda has been restrained by the democracy, by the inertia and slow pace of the law and by the dynamics of capitalism. Nevertheless, with good reason the values and views of this class have been perceived as the wave of the future, which others may resist or slow down, but which they must somehow adjust to.

Organized religion is a cultural institution par excellence; it would have been surprising indeed if it had not been drawn into the *Kulturkampf.* The mainline Protestant churches were sucked into it from the beginning. Inevitably, they reflected the cultural break lines, and with a vengeance. In not a single denomination, of course, are members of the new middle class a majority. But the clergy and the officials of the mainline churches belong to the new middle class by virtue of their education, their associations and their "reference group." It is here that the dynamics of bureaucracy took over from the dynamics of class. The former reflects what Roberto Michels called the "iron law of oligarchy" — the ability of a bureaucracy to

106

maintain itself even against the will of a majority of constituents and their elected representatives. In denomination after denomination, people who represented the new culture took over the bureaucratic machinery and thus the public face of the community. Bishops and other traditional authorities were unable to understand let alone to stop this process. As to the laity, contrary to what some observers expected, it did not put up a fight either. Few people in mainline churches want to invest time and energy in ecclesiastical infighting; this is not why they go to church. Instead, laypeople voted with their pocketbooks and their feet: they reduced their contributions and, in large numbers, they left. As a result, all the mainline churches have been suffering from both a fiscal and a demographic hemorrhage. Both conditions are still critical, though one may expect them to stabilize at some point. Likely, a residue of denominational loyalty by some plus an adherence to the new values by others will ensure that none of these churches will disappear completely. What is more, because these churches so comform to the prevailing elite culture, the general public will continue to perceive them as the mainline.

To a considerable extent the evangelical resurgence since the mid-1970s developed as a "resistance movement" against the new culture. Its clientele has been mainly lower-middle- and working-class, relatively uneducated, heavily provincial. Through its size, evangelicalism has been able to achieve a number of political and ecclesiastical successes (such as in the role of the new Christian right in some recent elections or in the takeover of the Southern Baptist Convention). All the same, here too the cultural battle is unequal. These communities, even more than business, lack the institutions and the know-how to mount an effective cultural resistance. Their very social and political successes are their undoing, as they are sucked into the ambience of the national culture. As James Davison Hunter has shown, the values of the other side are growing within evangelical Protestantism in exact measure as its members become better educated and upwardly mobile. And as recent survey data suggest, the growth of evangelicalism has been the result of demography, not conversion: Southern Baptists have more children than Episcopalians, and disgruntled Episcopalians are more likely to become unchurched than to become evangelicals. The net gain of the emigration of mainline Protestants from their churches is, therefore, likely to accrue to secularization rather than to evangelicalism. As to the Roman Catholic community, it has been buffeted by the same social and cultural forces, especially since Vatican II (probably inevitably) greatly weakened the institutional defenses against the overall culture. Here too the "iron law of oligarchy" has been brilliantly in evidence, much to the bewilderment of the bishops. There are, of course, two important differences as against Protestantism. The Roman Catholic Church is an international and an authoritarian organization. Both its internationalism and its authoritarianism have also been weakened by the post–Vatican II reforms, but they are still enough of a reality to make it unlikely that American Roman Catholicism will lose its distinctiveness in the way that, for example, American Lutheranism did in the wake of the recent merger.

To return to mainline Protestantism, the sociological picture is quite clear. Its churches are dwindling in numbers, but their allegiance to the ascendant middle-class culture will probably guarantee their continued public role. This culture is highly secularized. The mainline churches will thus contribute in a double way to the secularization of America — by legitimating a set of highly secularized values and by contributing to the unchurched population through its emigrants. The public face of these churches will continue to be shaped by an officialdom that faithfully reflects the interests and the culture of the new middle class. The former are likely to be fairly stable — interests are more perduring than cultural fashions — and thus the political orientation of these churches will continue to be liberal. The ideological expressions of these interests, though, are likely to vary even while, broadly speaking, they remain left-leaning. It is likely that the worldwide collapse of socialism will moderate some of the more extreme leftist sentiments in these quarters (though there is always some unlikely Third World country that these people will look to as, at long last, embodying "true socialism").

At the moment, as previously mentioned, feminism is the prevailing orthodoxy, which is why "inclusive language" (which serves to stigmatize and exclude those who dissent from the orthodoxy) is pushed with such vehemence. Environmentalism and other forms of Green ideology may catch up. And other, though as yet invisible, doctrines and movements may come to command center stage. What is most unlikely to change is the underlying structure of these cultural interactions: the ideologies and agendas of the churches all originate outside them; the churches play a basically passive role in the cultural drama, as receptors and disseminators rather than as initiators; they "read the signs of the times." It does not seem to occur to them that they might *write* them. In all of this, the church-society and church-culture relationships of mainline Protestantism have not changed at all from the situation I described in *The Noise of Solemn Assemblies*. Now, as then, these are middle-class institutions, legitimating middle-class interests and values. It just happens that the American middle class has changed. The "assemblies" are the same, if you will (and more "solemn" than ever); the "noise," to be sure, has changed.

Sociological understanding is a far cry from moral and theological assessment. Morally, the new middle-class culture is a mixed bag, as was the old middle-class culture and indeed every human culture this side of the kingdom. There is a strong continuity between the two cultures in their self-righteousness and their propensity to engage in potentially fanatical crusades; these are morally unattractive features indeed. The new middle class, I would argue, has a number of morally positive features, especially in its attitudes toward race and toward ethnic or other cultural differences; it is a racially and ethnically tolerant culture, and this is good. I would also agree, up to a point, with its self-assessment as a liberating force against the overly repressive features of an earlier bourgeois culture. I agree that a certain measure of hedonism was a good thing to inject into American middle-class Puritanism, and the latter's sexual mores were indeed a bit oppressive (though not at all as oppressive as the would-be liberators pretended). In this context one should make special mention of the earlier attitudes toward homosexuals. One need not subscribe to all the rewriting of history by the gay movement to agree that the treatment of homosexuality in Anglo-Saxon Protestant culture was barbaric; the change has on the whole been for the better. On the negative side of the ledger one must charge the new middle-class culture with a formidable list of moral aberrations, such as the mindless endorsement of faraway tyrannies or terrorist movements as long as these could be thought of as being "on the right side of history," the equally mindless endorsement of all types of domestic radicalisms from the Black Panthers to Greenpeace, the insouciant acceptance of millions of abortions as simply an expression of the right to choose, not to mention the other (less tangible) damage done to many lives by the brash social engineering of new middle-class professionals (for instance, in education). The old bourgeoisie was by no means the wonderful world that conservatives nostalgically make it out to be; the new bourgeoisie, in my opinion, is even less wonderful. In terms of *what* the churches have been legitimating, there has been a considerable degree of moral slippage.

Theologically, if one momentarily brackets the moral question, I see no difference between the old situation and the new. In both cases there has been an all-too-easy identification of Christian faith with sets of secular values and secular agendas. This was a distortion of the gospel then, as it is a distortion now. Needless to say, the distortion becomes even more disturbing if one removes the moral brackets: Making the American flag into a quasi-sacramental object is offensive; doing the same with the banner of this or that movement of murderous totalitarianism is loathsome. Yet one must always be cognizant that at no moment in its two millennia of history has the

Christian church been free of such aberrations and distortions. It would be extraordinarily ahistorical to ascribe some special propensity toward apostasy to present-day churches. The gravity with which one views the present situation will also depend on one's ecclesiology. The question is how seriously one takes the public face of the churches. I'm unsure about this.

I'm well aware that in many hundreds of local congregations the gospel is being effectively preached, the sacraments are being reverently administered, people are praying and getting answers to their prayers, and the sick, the sorrowful and the dying are being consoled — and all this without any regard for the busy activities and pronouncements emanating from national headquarters. I find this reflection comforting, especially as I know a few such congregations. My comfort is disturbed, however, when I reflect further that the same could have been said about many local parishes at the time of the Borgias and this could have suggested that the Reformation was a totally unnecessary exercise. The public face of the churches does matter because the Christian church, by its very mission, must be a public institution. Christianity, as we frequently hear, is not just a personal, private affair. It constitutes a community, which has a historical and a social location. National headquarters matter, and they must be taken seriously — perhaps more seriously than they take themselves, for it is the face of Christ that is being publicly distorted.

The church will survive until the Lord returns. In its worship today — even where that worship is weak or warped — the church participates in the eternal liturgy of all creation. Nothing can change this. The historical course of any particular Christian community, such as that of mainline Protestantism, is of only limited significance in that perspective. For a Christian this is a reassuring thought: it puts all mundane concerns in proportion; it encourages one to follow one's own vocation and leave all outcomes to the Lord of history.

My own vocation is in the world; I try to exercise it responsibly. The developments in mainline Protestantism discussed here, and more especially the developments within the Lutheran community, have made me ecclesiastically homeless. I don't relish this condition; I can live with it. This need be of no particular interest to others, except for one observation: Despite various unique aspects of my own biography, my problems in this matter are not unique. I consider myself theologically liberal, at least in the sense that I would find it quite impossible to move into any branch of evangelicalism and almost as impossible to move toward Rome. At the same time, for carefully weighed reasons (almost all of them based on my understanding of the world as a social scientist), I cannot give assent to the left-liberal-liberationist politics that has become monopolistically established in nonevangelical Protestantism. In the latter milieu, in most places, someone like me can only be, at best, tolerated and marginalized. People like me are many. They find themselves stranded between two equally unacceptable fundamentalisms, the one theological, the other moral and political. This is obviously uncomfortable for them, but it also offers little comfort for anyone with responsibility for the future of American Protestantism.

I have not exactly fulfilled my assignment. I have not reported on how my mind has changed in the past decade. In my business I must come up with hypotheses all the time, many of which are subsequently falsified by the empirical evidence. Changing one's mind as a social scientist is both an occupational hazard and a point of professional honor. Perhaps I can rise to the assignment by one final observation. Ten years ago or so I believed there was a good chance that a group of committed individuals might yet reverse the Babylonian captivity to the Zeitgeist of contemporary Protestant Christendom. I see no evidence of such a turn. At least speaking sociologically, then, I have changed my mind about that. Speaking theologically, of course, such an assessment provides no alibi for giving up. Sociology cannot predict the movements of the Holy Spirit. All we can do is to follow our callings.

Robert N. Bellah

Finding the Church:
Post-Traditional Discipleship

In 1970 I published an intellectual autobiography that served as the introduction to my collection of essays titled *Beyond Belief: Essays on Religion in a Post-Traditional World*. I want to make a first effort at bringing that essay up to date. I will, however, take two essays I published in the 1970s (both included in *Beyond Belief*) as intellectual benchmarks with respect to which I will measure changes, developments and continuities in the subsequent years. They are "Religious Evolution" and "Civil Religion in America," the two most influential essays I ever wrote. I want to trace the development of my thought with regard to discipleship and citizenship from the positions set forth in those essays and largely reiterated in the introduction to Beyond Belief.

The essay "Religious Evolution" was more Hegelian, more ethnocentric and more personal than I realized when I wrote it. The religious *Weltgeist* turned out to be the *Geist* of my own culture, as indicated by the special prominence of Protestant-

---

Robert N. Bellah is professor of sociology at the University of California at Berkeley.

ism — virtually the only instance of the stage of "Early Modern Religion." It also turned out to be the *Geist* of myself in stage five, "Modern Religion," as is evident to me from the title, *Beyond Belief,* with its subtitle alluding to the "post-traditional." What I was celebrating in what I called modern religion was a degree of freedom from traditional and institutional restraints which curiously prefigures several of the "post" movements of recent years (indeed, in 1970 I already referred to the contemporary situation as "postmodern"). In my description, modern religion focused on the individual, who had the task of largely making up his or her religion from whatever traditional or current materials lay at hand, finding like-minded individuals to cooperate in this effort if they were available. Radical voluntarism was the key, although I never failed to moderate it with statements to the effect that freedom could be exercised only "within [largely unspecified] limits."

Readers of *Habits of the Heart* will probably recognize that in the 1960s I was championing just the sort of religious individualism, strongly identified with "expressive individualism," that came in for rather severe treatment in the later book. Obviously by 1985 I had "changed my mind." It is difficult at this point to sort out the cultural, political and personal changes that can account for this difference in my position, but I will try.

As I recounted in *Beyond Belief,* I was reconverted to Christianity in the middle 1950s by Paul Tillich — first by *The Courage to Be,* and then by his sermons and other books and by some degree of personal contact when we were both at Harvard in the late '50s and early '60s. But I was in a quandary as to how to give institutional expression to my new situation, and with my essentially individualistic position, in no hurry to do anything about it. Since Tillich's preaching was so incomparable, I felt that no form of worship that focused on the sermon was going to be satisfactory to me. Early on I felt my only options were silence or liturgy. I tried attending Episcopal morning prayer on several occasions but found it excessively dry.

During the mid-'60s I established a loose connection with the Cambridge Friends Meeting and even taught First Day School at the junior-high level for a while, something I found far more exhausting than my teaching at Harvard. Although I shared many of the social concerns of the Cambridge Friends and came to admire the spiritual depth of some of the members, the silence I was seeking was all too often broken, sometimes with anecdotes from the latest issue of *Reader's Digest*. After my move to Berkeley in 1967 I put the institutional question on hold and was, when I wrote the introduction, essentially a "private Christian," even though I knew at some level of consciousness that that was an oxymoron.

In the late '70s I made my second approach to the Episcopal Church, this time at Saint Mark's Church in Berkeley. By then the main Sunday service was no longer morning prayer, but the Eucharist. I think that was quite important to me, but also Saint Mark's was a wonderful parish, described pseudonymously as "Saint Stephen's" in Chapter 9 of *Habits of the Heart*.

I do not look happily on my 25 years of shopping for the right parish; I have been quite hard on consumer Christians who flit from church to church seeking the most convenient services. But it is unrealistic to assume that Christians today will stay where they were brought up, if they were religiously brought up at all. Both the Protestant principle of voluntarism and the modern respect for autonomous decision make it natural for adults to choose their own religious affiliation. Here I would adopt the analogy of Hegel's conception of marriage, namely, that it is a contract to enter a noncontractual relation. It is a contract in that it is entered into freely. It is noncontractual in that it is in intention indissoluble. Hegel, a devoted Lutheran, allowed for divorce on the grounds that we are sinners and may not be able to live up to our intention, but the intention is never to be taken lightly.

Even though my church identity did not finally clarify until the past ten or 12 years, I feel it is no longer an open question for me. I suppose there might be developments in my parish or my denomination or myself that might cause me to change, but they would have to be drastic indeed to undermine what I now consider a settled commitment. In any case I hope never again to be cut off from the body of Christ in the concrete sociological meaning of that term. A period of seeking, when one tries out various options, would seem normal in our kind of society, but I would not recommend my protracted process.

One of the things that brought me back to a more active churchmanship by the end of the '70s was the fact that what I had been writing and publishing gained for me a growing religious audience. Not only was I asked to speak to religious groups, from local congregations to denominational assemblies, but I was even asked to preach — at a time when I had no church affiliation. This situation made me feel increasingly inauthentic. The church was calling me to be in fact what I was experimenting with in my writing. The point I want to underscore here is that I did not undergo an existential decision to "return to religion" out of the pure innerness of my personal situation. Even my initial shift in point of view that allowed me as an adult to consider religion as a viable option came from my exposure to Tillich and his confident assertion that Christianity is not "belief in the unbelievable." And my later turn to more active fellowship in the company of believers was motivated as much by a feeling that the church had need of me as it was by any private needs of my own.

Having said something as to the development of my discipleship, let me now take up the question of citizenship. From my adolescence to the late '50s I had been quite alienated, both culturally and politically, from American society. My decision as an undergraduate to major in social anthropology and as a graduate student to study East Asia, especially Japan, had to do with my desire to understand societies quite different from my own — tribal societies like the Pueblos and the Navahos, or an exotic civilization like Japan — where I could feel a degree of cultural authenticity that I did not experience at home. My Marxist political involvements as an undergraduate made me vulnerable, during the McCarthy period, to pressures that made me decide to go to Canada in 1955. For a while I did not know if I would ever return, but after the hysteria abated I was appointed to the Harvard faculty in 1957.

My year in Japan in 1960-61 had the effect of reminding me how American I was, even though I deeply appreciated the experience of Japan. As part of my Fulbright obligations I gave a series of lectures in Japanese universities on religion in American public life that formed the germ of the later essay on civil religion. The early '60s were also an optimistic time at home when it seemed that the civil rights movement was bringing about long overdue changes in our society and a new phase of democratization seemed possible.

My more positive attitude toward my own country was rather abruptly shocked by our involvement in Vietnam, which I knew at once was a terrible mistake. When I was induced in 1965 to write an essay for an issue of *Daedalus* on religion in America, I chose the theme of religion in American public life, concluding with a ringing condemnation of the Vietnam war. That was the essay published in 1967 as "Civil Religion in America," which in important respects changed my life. The response it generated was far greater than anything I had ever published before. In order to respond to the many invitations to write and speak stimulated by the essay, I had to give myself a quick course in American studies, something I had almost consciously avoided hitherto. Here, as in my work on the church — and the audiences were to an extent overlapping — my concerns were at the same time practical and intellectual. I felt that I could not withdraw from my new American audience and return to my chosen field of Japanese studies if my fellow citizens found what I had to say interesting and helpful at a time when my country's actions cried out for public involvement.

In 1973 I gave the lectures (at Hebrew Union College in Cincinnati) that would be published as *The Broken Covenant* in 1975, and would in turn project me into an intensive year of public speaking during the 1976 Bicentennial. But when the subject of civil religion became a minor academic industry, I became increasingly concerned, as conferences, panels and symposia on the subject proliferated, that the whole issue was bogging down into arguments over definition and that substance was being overlooked. What was particularly distressing to me was the almost inveterate tendency in some quarters to identify what I called civil religion with the idolatrous worship of the state. Since I had, from my initial article, emphasized the element of divine judgment over the nation, quoting the great lines from Lincoln's Second Inaugural Address as my central text, I could not but find such an interpretation abhorrent. It was not that I failed to recognize the existence of such idolatrous belief, though historically it was more commonly enunciated by preachers than by politicians, but that I believed it to be a perversion of the central and normative tradition. It was as if those who would be quite shocked if the essence of Christianity were judged by the faith's most perverse historical expressions had no qualms in doing just that to American civil religion.

In any case my own concerns were not definitional or even theoretical so much as they were practical. *The Broken Covenant* was indeed a jeremiad intended to change America, and of course it was widely received that way. But it did not put a stop to the definitional disputes, and by 1980 I was ready to drop the term. *Varieties of Civil Religion,* a collection of essays published in that year by Phillip Hammond and myself, turned out to be my swan song with respect to civil religion. In my introduction I suggested that the religio-political problem was endemic in all cultures whether something like the American civil religion existed or not. And though the book had several essays concerned with the U.S., it turned resolutely in a comparative direction as the most hopeful way of dealing with the larger issues.

In *Habits of the Heart* (1985) the term "civil religion" does not appear. Instead my four coauthors and I speak of "the biblical and republican traditions," which we do not claim to be identical but which we see as deeply interrelated. We support a contemporary reappropriation of them over against the radical individualism, in utilitarian and expressive form, that seemed in recent years to be driving the older traditions to the periphery of our culture. In retrospect this terminological decision seems wise, for in all the discussion which *Habits* generated, which was sometimes quite vituperative, the issues remained substantive and not definitional.

Habits is a political book. It is also, and only a little less obviously, a religious book. It was explicitly public philosophy; it was (largely) implicitly public theology. Barbara Ehrenreich picked up the cue, even if she misinterpreted it, when she questioned in her review in the *Nation* how "five atheistic social scientists" could counsel Americans to go to church. Of course we did not counsel people to go to church, though we did try to show why some of the people we interviewed do go to church and what the meaning of the biblical tradition is in America. What Ehrenreich could not imagine is that the five authors of *Habits* were all active members of their respective religious communities; she assumed — and statistically she would be right in her assumption — that we would be atheists.

Some readers have misread *Habits* as a Protestant book. Others, reading more carefully, noted its differences from *The Broken Covenant* and the degree to which *Habits* was not a jeremiad. Some even found it optimistic, though optimism and pessimism are in the eye of the beholder. Actually I was the only WASP in the *Habits* group; three of my coauthors were raised Catholic and one is Jewish. The difference is as much in tone as in content. Whereas *The Broken Covenant* was the voice of a prophet crying in the wilderness, alternately denouncing and lamenting for his people, *Habits* and its successor volume *The Good Society,* written by the same five authors and to be published in 1991, speak as one group of citizens to our fellow citizens, criticizing some things but also encouraging, offering examples of effective citizenship and church membership, and looking forward, if not with optimism, at least with hope. Instead of an individual voice, we speak from within a community (actually many communities, but first of all the community of the five authors) to others in overlapping communities that finally include the whole earth.

If *The Broken Covenant* is an expression of Tillich's Protestant principle, then the more recent work, with its emphasis on the common good and, if one reads just below the surface, the body of Christ, is an expression of what he called the catholic principle. I do not mean to imply that our emphasis is exclusive, for we intend, both politically and religiously, to be ecumenical. And on the whole we have been received as such.

To break down the boundaries: that was our hope, and with the great political changes of 1989 and 1990 the possibilities seem greater than we had imagined. Yet the barriers are numerous, and to encourage a genuinely synoptic discipleship and citizenship is a task that still faces many obstacles. With the publication of *The Good Society* the collaborative phase of my work will be over, and I hope to return again to the problems raised in my essay on religious evolution nearly three decades ago.

Discipleship and citizenship and the relation between them have been my enduring preoccupations. The problem of meaning is inextricably related to the problem of what must be done, but they are not identical problems and one must move back and forth between them.

The university is not the most comfortable place to carry out either of these kinds of inquiry in the present age. Specialization proliferates in the research university, and normative questions find no obvious disciplinary home. Even so, the spirit of the academic community as a moral community, or, as Josiah Royce put it, a community of interpreters, is not entirely dead. Indeed, here, too, there are some unexpectedly hopeful signs. In the border areas between philosophy, the humanities and the social sciences there are some significant openings. Books such as Alasdair MacIntyre's *After Virtue*, Albert Borgmann's *Technology and the Character of Contemporary Life*, Stephen Toulmin's *Cosmopolis*, Charles Taylor's *Sources of the Self*, and

Theodore Von Laue's *World Revolution of Westernization* cannot be neatly pigeonholed in any discipline, and all of them are full of implications for theology. Perhaps not since the generation of the classic American philosophers — Pierce, Royce, James, Dewey and Mead (none of them technical philosophers in the contemporary meaning of the term) — has it been possible to range so broadly over the great intellectual issues of the day and break the taboo that would separate religion from secular culture. These developments are stimulated and encouraged by parallel developments in Europe — as for instance in the great synthesizing intelligence of Jürgen Habermas.

It is apparent, even in these few lines, what I owe to Tillich, whose thought has so deeply penetrated my own that it would be very hard for me to specify all that I have learned from him. I was also fortunate to have as my principal teacher in sociology Talcott Parsons, a man of extraordinary intellectual range and openness. Although Talcott never wrote much about religion, sociology of religion was probably his greatest lecture course, one that we taught jointly for a while and one that I continue to teach in my own way up to the present. I have increasingly come to see H. Richard Niebuhr as an intellectual forebear, although I never met him and did not begin to study him seriously until after his death. Like Tillich and Parsons, Niebuhr ranged between religion, the social sciences and the humanities in a most fruitful way. It was Niebuhr who continued the tradition of Royce and Mead into the second half of the 20th century, when the philosophers had largely forgotten them.

These reflections on the major early influences on my thinking have an obvious bearing on where I am trying to go in my remaining years of intellectual inquiry. I do not mean, by the few references possible in this article, to suggest any kind of canon. I have been deeply influenced by East Asian classical culture, tribal societies and their myths, and feminists and liberationists among contemporary thinkers, all of whom I would include in the ongoing conversation. If it is to certain European and American thinkers of the past that I recur, it is not with their canonized texts that I am concerned, but with their aspirations, their willingness to deal with the largest questions of meaning and responsible action in a free society. Western theology has been accused of marginalizing and excluding too many voices, some of whom are now fortunately beginning to be heard. But theology itself has been marginalized and excluded from the research university, with damaging consequences for our intellectual life and the education of our young people. It will not be easy to change that situation, but I am happy to join those who are trying to do so.

So I move back and forth between fundamental questions of meaning and the problem of responsible action in a democratic society. The latter problem is particularly salient for Americans in a period when we have watched world democratic revolutions on TV. Given the resonance of world events, I will be surprised if Americans, too, are not before long swept up into the process of reconsidering our inherited institutions and their consequences for our life today. Nations, even very powerful nations, no longer have the power to control their own fate. They are affected not only by economic pressures but by cultural pressures. If the pressure toward globalization of our thinking in practical matters continues to increase, as it almost inevitably will, it can only intensify the spiritual questions that our common fate on this earth raises in new and urgent ways. It is, I believe, the primary task of the intellectual today, with all due modesty, to attempt to mediate these practical, intellectual and spiritual pressures so that we can hand on our material and moral endowment to future generations with some degree of hope.

In the end I am not sure whether I have "changed my mind" or not. The questions and the aspirations show a remarkable continuity. The answers and the dialogue partners have changed, sometimes drastically, but that is how a living tradition works. So I will end on a somewhat ironic note of contrast: in 1970 I wrote of a "post-traditional world"; today I believe that only living traditions make it possible to have a world at all.

Thomas C. Oden

Then and Now: The Recovery of Patristic Wisdom

Then and *now* have specific autobiographical meanings in what follows. "Then" means the period of my personal development before I became immersed in the meeting with and study of the ecumenical councils and leading ancient consensual exegetes. "Now" means what has been happening since that meeting became a serious matter for me in the mid-'70s. "Consensual exegetes" are Athanasius, Basil, Gregory Nazianzen and Chrysostom in the East and Ambrose, Jerome, Augustine and Gregory the Great in the West.

If I rhetorically exaggerate differences between then and now, shaped as I am by present passions, my intent is to describe major reversals between then and now without allowing them to die the death of a thousand qualifications. I am not disavowing my former social idealism, but rather celebrating it as having been taken up into a more inclusive understanding of history and humanity.

The pivot occurred when my irascible, endearing Jewish

Thomas C. Oden teaches at Drew University Theological School, Madison, New Jersey.

mentor, the late Will Herberg, straightforwardly told me what Protestant friends must have been too polite to say, that I would remain uneducated until I had read deeply in patristic and medieval writers. That was in the early '70s, when with long hair, bobbles, bangles and beads and a gleam of communitarian utopianism in my eyes, I finally found my way into the fourth-century treatise by Nemesius, *peri phuseos anthropon* ("On the Nature of the Human"), where it at length dawned on me that ancient wisdom could be the basis for a deeper critique of modern narcissistic individualism than I had yet seen. If you had asked me then what my life would look like now, I would have guessed completely wrong. It now seems that life is more hedged by grace and providence than I once imagined.

I now revel in the mazes and mysteries of perennial theopuzzles: Can God be known? Does God care? Why did God become human? Is Jesus the Christ? How could he be tempted yet without sin? If Father, Son and Spirit, how is God one? How does freedom cooperate with grace? How can the community of celebration both express the holiness of the body of Christ in the world and at the same time engage in the radical transformation of the world? How is it possible daily to refract the holiness of God within the history of sin? How shall I live my present life in relation to final judgment? Not a new question on the list, nor a dull one.

Then I fancied I was formulating totally unprecedented issues and ordering them in an original way. Later while reading John of Damascus on the *oikonomia* of God (in *The Orthodox Faith*) I began belatedly to learn that the reordering of theology I thought I was just inventing (the sequence now shaping *Systematic Theology*) had been well understood as a received tradition in the eighth century. All my supposedly new questions were much investigated amid the intergenerational wisdom of the *communio sanctorum*. It was while reading Chrysostom on voluntary poverty that I realized that Peter Berger's sociological theory of knowledge elites had long ago been intuited. It was while reading Cyril of Jerusalem's *Catechetical Lecture* on evidences for the resurrection that I became persuaded that Pannenberg had provided a more accurate account than Bultmann of the resurrection. It was while reading the fourth-century figure Macrina and the women surrounding Jerome that I realized how profoundly women had influenced monastic and ascetic disciplines. It was while reading in Augustine's *City of God* of the ironic providences of history that I realized how right was Solzhenitsyn on the spiritual promise of Russia. And so it went.

Then focused on interpersonal humanistic psychology, now personal reflection is occurring in the light of the theandric (God-man) One in whom our humanity is most completely realized. Then blown by every wind of doctrine and preoccupied with fads and the ethos of hypertoleration, now I suffer fools a little less gladly.

What has shifted in my scholarly investigation between then and now? Psychologically the shift has been away from Freudian, Rogerian and Nietzschean values, especially individualistic self-actualization and narcissistic self-expression, and toward engendering durable habits of moral excellence and covenant community; methodologically, away from modern culture-bound individuated experience and toward the shared public texts of Scripture and ecumenical tradition; politically, away from trust in regulatory power and rationalistic planning to historical reasoning and a relatively greater critical trust in the responsible free interplay of interests in the marketplace of goods and ideas.

Now I experience wider cross-cultural freedom of inquiry into and within the variables of Christian orthodoxy mediated through brilliant Christian voices of other times and places. Now I experience a liberation for orthodoxy in the endless flexibility of centered apostolic teaching to meld with different cultural environments while offering anew the eternal word of the theandric, messianic Servant in each new historical setting. Then I was seeking to live out my life mostly in accountability to contemporary academic peers; now awareness of final judg-

ment makes me only proximately and semiseriously account-
able to peers.

My trajectory changed because of a simple hermeneutical
reversal: Before the mid-'70s I had been steadily asking questions on the hidden premise of four key value assumptions of
modern consciousness: hedonic self-actualization, autonomous
individualism, reductive naturalism and moral relativism. Now
my questions about decaying modernity are being shaped by
ancient, consensual, classic Christian exegesis of holy writ. The
history of Christianity is a history of exegesis whose best interpretations are offered by those most simply seeking to state the
mind of the believing community. Then I was using the biblical
text instrumentally, sporadically and eisegetically to support my
modern ideological commitments. Now the Bible is asking my
questions more deeply than I ever could before. Then mildly
contemptuous of patristic exegesis, now I thrive on patristic
and matristic texts and wisdom. Now I am at every level seeking
guidance in the written word as ecumenically received and con-
sensually exegeted. Now when I teach my brightest graduate
students, I have nothing better to offer than the written word
as viewed through the unfolding meeting of brilliant and con-
senting minds in time with that written word (Athanasius, Ambrose and company). Now I preach less about my own sentiments and opinions and more from testimony canonically
received and grasped by the believing community of all times
and places, trusting that seed will bear fruit in its own time and
that word will address these hearers without too much static
from me.

While reading Vincent of Lérins's fifth-century aids to remembering *(Commonitory)* I gained the essential hermeneutical
foothold in defining ecumenical teaching under the threefold
test of catholicity as "that which has been believed everywhere,
always, and by all" *(quod ubique, quod semper, quod ab omnibus
creditum est)*. From then on it was a straightforward matter of
searching modestly to identify those teachings.

I have learned nothing more valuable than confessing my

own sin honestly and receiving God's mercy daily. Meanwhile I curb pretenses of originality and listen intently to those who attest a tradition of general lay consent.

I do not mean by "then" that I was unconverted or lacking faith in God; rather, I was lacking attentiveness to apostolic testimony and the sanctification of time through grace. I do not mean that now I have ceased being a modern man or become bored with secularization. The world has become ever more alive to me because of the seed of the Word being planted in this fallow soil of the decaying wastes of modernity.

Then I was always on the edge of theological boredom; now no trivial pursuits. Among theological issues most deeply engaging me in the past year are sin in believers, the virginal conception of the Lord, providence in history, prevenient grace, the holiness, catholicity and apostolicity of the one church, radical judgment at the end of history and the rejection of sin by atoning grace.

Then I distrusted anything that faintly smelled of orthodoxy. Now I relish studying the rainbow of orthodox testimonies and happily embrace the term paleo-orthodoxy if for no other reason than to signal clearly that I do not mean modern neo-orthodoxy. Now I am experiencing a refreshing sense of classic theological liberation. Paleo-orthodoxy understands itself to be postlib, postmodern, postfundy, postneoanything, since the further one "progresses" from ancient apostolic testimony the more hopeless the human condition becomes.

As a Protestant I grow daily more catholic without experiencing any diminution of myself as evangelical. When my path becomes strewn with thorny epithets like fundy or cryptopapist or byzantine or (my favorite) "Protestantism's most Catholic theologian," I feel like I just got a badge of honor. I do not mind being charged by conservative Protestants with drawing too near Rome, for that only opens up an urgent and significant dialogue. I sometimes find myself in the comic position of publicly debating liberal Catholics and suddenly realizing that they are consorting with the old liberal Protestant strumpets of my seedy past, while I am setting forth their own traditional arguments from their magisterium. I grow daily in appreciation of what traditionally grounded Catholics can do for Protestant evangelicals and charismatics, who need their solidity and teaching tradition in order to have something to bounce off of and even at times fight. Now I find few questions in modern society that are not dealt with more thoughtfully in *Osservatore Romano* than in *National Catholic Reporter* or *Christianity and Crisis.* Then I was a regular reader of journals forever commending accommodation to modernity; now I am drawn to the tough-love countercultural criticism of *Communio, First Things, New Oxford Review* and *Thirty Days.* Among those I most admire are John Paul II, Cardinal Joseph Ratzinger, Solzhenitsyn and the mother of Gorbachev.

My shift from then to now is from a fixation on modernity to the steady flow of postmodern paleo-orthodox consciousness. Postmodern does not mean ultramodern. What some call postmodern is an already-dated expression of the last gasps of modernity, an ultramodern phase in its dying throes. We are already living in a postmodern era, but it is not the postmodernity being described by those who fly that flag (the unhappy campers following Derrida, Foucault and the deconstructionist "Posties"). The after-deconstructionist good news is that the disillusionments of the illusions of modernity are already being corrected by classical Christian teaching. They are also being corrected by conservative and orthodox Jewish consciousness, the best traditions of Islam and ancient Hindu and Buddhist teaching. The return to classic forms of religious consciousness is the hope of the deteriorating modern situation, the source of its most profound critique and the practical basis for living through and transcending its identity-diffusion, discontent, moral relativism and frenetic quest for relevance. The reason I am now trying to write almost nothing that is currently relevant is that tomorrow it will be less relevant. I am seeking to understand what is perennially true, not what is ephemerally relevant.

No current moral issue is more deep-going than the acid

destructiveness of modernity. No political project is more urgent for society than the recovery of classic Christian consciousness through the direct address of texts of Scripture and tradition. There is nothing better I can do for the moral dilemmas of our time than offer undiluted the ancient wisdom of the community of celebration. From that singleminded decision, everything else has followed. I am only reporting what has very gradually, silently and unspectacularly happened: a slow metamorphosis that still looks slightly ugly to old friends who want me to be more like my old radical-activist self.

You may wonder how this reversal has redefined my moral and political commitments. This quiet theological work is more effective politically because less entangled with partisan biases and immediate interests. Then I was devoutly and sentimentally attached to a particular wing of a political party. Now with broken wing I walk more freely through the wide open fields of political options I could not have imagined myself considering a few years ago. Now chastened and somewhat more aware of the transpolitical nature of ordination, I am learning belatedly (out of the countercultural tradition from Polycarp to Menno Simons) some measure of political repentance, mostly in the form of silence, after sinning much politically. That itself is a vast political decision, to turn from partisanship toward political engagement along different lines: teaching the written word. Now I experience greater freedom to attest the received text and let the chips fall. Offering word and sacrament to penitents with conflicting and ambivalent political understandings is quite different now than when I pretended I had some superior political gnosis.

Some may counter that I am just growing quite a bit older, which I am grateful not to have to deny. I am waist-deep in middle age, with three grown kids, all delightful friends very different from Edrita and me — having negotiated the hazards of postmodern history without crippling effects. For those who might have wondered about my physical condition, I did have open-heart surgery in July of 1989 followed by a myocardial infarction and a second surgery all on the same day — they cleaned out the old pipes and replaced a few — but within a month of that ordeal I was walking ten miles a day, and now, in the best physical shape I have been in for years, I am running 12 miles a week, so no one need be overly concerned. Through this brush with death my awareness of how God's strength is made perfect through human weakness has deepened. To my significant other, the courageous woman who has accompanied me for 38 years of this journey, I am incalculably grateful; without her I cannot imagine where I might be — probably not here, maybe not anywhere.

I want to be permitted to study the unchanging God without something else to do, some pragmatic reason or result. This is what I most want to do theologically: simply enjoy the study of God, not write about it, view it in relation to its political residue or pretentiously imagine that it will have some social effect. The joy of inquiry into God is a sufficient end in itself.

Some dear old friends know how to ask me only one question: Why are you merely studying God? Why aren't you out there with "our side" on the streets making "significant changes"? — which usually means the imagined revolutions of introverted knowledge elites. Plain theology is wonderful enough in its very acts of thinking, reading, praying, communing and uniting with the body — not for its effects, its written artifacts or its social consequences, though it has these. Spirit-blessed theology is not merely a means to an end of social change, though I can think of no action that has more enduring political significance. The study of God is to be enjoyed for its own unique subject: the One most beautiful of all, most worthy to be praised.

I relish those half days when nothing else is scheduled, when I have no worldly responsibilities but to engage in this quiet dialogue which I understand as my vocation. It is not something I must do or have to do or am required to do, but am free to do. Summer is juicy, and a sabbatical leave is a foretaste of the celestial city. Why? Because I can do what I am

cut out to do. Not write, but think. The writing is only a means
to clarify my thinking.

When there is nothing on my calendar and I can do what
I want, I readpray, studypray, work (so it seems) pray, thinkpray,
just because there is nothing else better to do and nothing I
want more to do. Then occasionally my old, pragmatic activist
friends say to me, But why are you not out there on the street
working to change the world? I answer, I am out there on the
street in the most serious way by being here with my books,
and if you see no connection there, then you have not understood my vocation. I do not love the suffering poor less by
offering them what they need more.

We have lived through a desperate game: the attempt to
find some modern ideology, psychology or sociology that could
conveniently substitute for apostolic testimony. That game is all
over. We have no choice but to think about modernity amid the
collapse of modernity. We must reassess the role of historical
science amid the collapse of historical science. I do not despair
over modernity. I do celebrate the providence of God that works
amid premodern, modern and postmodern personal histories.
Most people I know are already living in a postmodern situation, though they may still worship the gods of modernity that
are every day being found to have clay feet.

The years of study that led to the four volumes of the
Classical Pastoral Care series and the study of Gregory the Great
(Pastoral Care in the Classic Tradition) helped free me to listen
to supposedly "precritical" writers with postcritical attentiveness. Now disappointed with the meager consequences of contemporary so-called "critical" scholarship — especially the biblical variety, with its ideological stridencies — I am more aware
of the resources for exegesis, pastoral care and spiritual formation that dwell quietly in the literature of the first five centuries
of the church, the mature period of the widely received exegetes,
the ecumenical teachers.

While some imagine postmodern paleo-orthodox Chris-
tianity to be precritical, I view it as postcritical. It is far too late

to be precritical if one has already spent most of one's life chasing the fecund rabbits of a supposed criticism based on the premises of modern chauvinism (that newer is always better; older, worse). One cannot be precritical after assimilating two centuries of modern naturalistic and idealistic criticism. If merely to use sources that emerged before a modern period some call "the age of criticism" is to be precritical, then in that sense I delight in being so. But note how damning that premise is to the integrity of modern criticism; it supposes that one is able to use only sources of one's own historical period. The controversy about modernity centers precisely on whether critical thinking belongs only to our own period. I believe it does not, while much that is called criticism continues to assume that it does. *After Modernity . . . What?*, a ten-year retrospect on *Agenda for Theology,* gave me a recent opportunity to state this critique of criticism more circumspectly.

Once hesitant to trust anyone over 30, now I hesitate to ᵗrust anyone under 300. I have found the late 17th century to be a reliable dividing line after which texts tend more to be corrupted by modernity. Once I thought it my solemn duty to read the *New York Times* almost every day; now, seldom. Why? It hinges on a "need to know" principle: I seem less to need to know all the news that is not quite fit to print than to know what Chrysostom taught about Galatians 2 or Basil on the Holy Spirit. The social and political events that are affecting my thinking are epic movements of despairing modernity, not discrete day-by-day scandal-sheet items like most of the supposed great media events of the past decade. Reading Amos ten times seems rather more important than the Sunday *Times* once. Take away all network TV and daily newspapers and give me cable stations C-Span, CNN and A&E, public radio and television, a remote channel selector, some shortwave radio, some heaped-up helpings of classical music, a decent evangelical radio station and a few weekly journals, and I have enough media blitz any given week.

I have watched my own oldline church tradition decline

during the era of the modern ecumenical movement in which I invested heavily. I have watched well-intended ecumenicity become twisted in the interest of 475 ideological assertions and public policy postures. My ecumenical commitment today is far more to ancient than to modern ecumenical teaching. The modern ecumenical movement has more than soured or failed; it has brought disaster and spiritual poverty in its wake. It is now time for the ancient ecumenical teaching to be recovered and show the way to a new formation of the one body of Christ embracing faithful Catholics, Protestants, evangelicals, Orthodox and charismatics. The day is gone when paternalistic oldline Protestant ecumenical advocates could easily claim the moral high ground.

After decades of well-meaning ecumania, I am unapologetically rediscovering my own theological tradition, especially its Eastern patristic and catholic taproots and Anglican-Puritan antecedents. The intriguing study that led me to edit *Phoebe Palmer: Selected Writings* for the Paulist Fathers' Sources of American Spirituality series has awakened in me a burning interest in the history of revivalism, British and American, particularly in its post–Phoebe Palmer holiness stages prior to Pentecostalism, a socially transforming evangelicalism quite different from that shaped by the inerrantist Princeton tradition.

I find it ironic that this *Century* series focuses on change while I steadily plod toward stability. The only thing that has changed from the old me is my steady growth toward orthodoxy and consensual, ancient classic Christianity, with its proximate continuity, catholicity and apostolicity. This implies my growing resistance to faddism, novelty, heresy, anarchism, antinomianism, pretensions of discontinuity, revolutionary talk and nonhistorical idealism.

When the Lord tore the kingdom of Israel from Saul, Samuel declared: "He who is the Glory of Israel does not lie or change his mind; for he is not a man, that he would change his mind" (1 Sam. 15:29). God's constant, attentive, holy love is eternally unchanging. Awakening gradually to the bright im-

Thomas C. Oden

mutability of God's responsive covenant love is precisely what has changed for me. Yahweh must have laughed in addressing the heirs of the old rascal Jacob with this ironic word: "I the Lord do not change. So you, O descendants of Jacob, are not destroyed" (Mal. 3:6). Still it is so: "Every good and perfect gift is from above, coming down from the Father of the heavenly lights, who does not change like shifting shadows" (James 1:17). But how difficult it would be to edit a series on "How My Mind Has Remained the Same."

Sallie McFague

An Earthly Theological Agenda

I teach a survey course in contemporary theology that covers the 20th century. When I took a similar course as a divinity student at Yale in the late '50s, it had considerable unity. We studied the great German theologians whose names began with "B" (seemingly a prerequisite for theological luminosity) — Barth, Bultmann, Brunner, Bonhoeffer — and, of course, Tillich. They were all concerned with the same issues, notably reason and revelation, faith and history, issues of methodology and, especially, epistemology: how can we *know* God?

More recent theology has no such unity. The first major shift came in the late '60s, with the arrival of the various liberation theologies, which are still growing and changing as more and different voices from the underside of history insist on being heard. While what separates these various theologies is great (much greater than what separated German theology and its American counterparts), one issue, at least, unites them: they ask not how we can know God but how we can change the world. We are now at the threshold of a second major shift in theological reflection during this century, a shift in which the

---

Sallie McFague is Carpenter Professor of Theology at Vanderbilt University in Nashville.

main issue will be not only how we can change the world but how we can save it from deterioration and its species from extinction.

The extraordinary events of the past year or so, with the simultaneous lessening of cold-war tensions and worldwide awakening to the consequences of human destruction of the flora and fauna and the ecosystem that supports them, signal a major change in focus. Perhaps it is more accurate to say that the focus of the liberation theologies widened to include, in addition to all oppressed human beings, all oppressed creatures as well as planet earth.

Liberation theologies insist rightly that all theologies are written from particular contexts. The one context which has been neglected and is now emerging is the broadest as well as the most basic: the context of the planet, a context which we all share and without which we cannot survive. It seems to me that this latest shift in 20th-century theology is not to a different issue from that of liberation theologies, but to a deepening of it, a recognition that the fate of the oppressed and the fate of the earth are inextricably interrelated, for we all live on one planet — a planet vulnerable to our destructive behavior.

The link between justice and ecological issues becomes especially evident in light of the dualistic, hierarchical mode of Western thought in which a superior and an inferior are correlated: male-female, white people–people of color, heterosexual-homosexual, able-bodied–physically challenged, culture-nature, mind-body, human-nonhuman. These correlated terms — most often normatively ranked — reveal clearly that domination and destruction of the natural world is inexorably linked with the domination and oppression of the poor, people of color, and all others that fall on the "inferior" side of the correlation. Nowhere is this more apparent than in the ancient and deep identification of women with nature, an identification so profound that it touches the very marrow of our being: our birth from the bodies of our mothers and our nourishment from the body of the earth. The power of nature — and of women — to give and withhold life epitomizes the inescapable connection between the two and thus the necessary relationship of justice and ecological issues. As many have noted, the status of women and of nature have been historically commensurate: as goes one, so goes the other.

A similar correlation can be seen between other forms of human oppression and a disregard for the natural world. Unless ecological health is maintained, for instance, the poor and others with limited access to scarce goods (due to race, class, gender or physical capability) cannot be fed. Grain must be grown for all to have bread. The characteristic Western mind-set has accorded intrinsic value, and hence duties of justice, principally to the upper half of the dualism and has considered it appropriate for those on the lower half to be used for the benefit of those on the upper. Western multinational corporations, for example, regard it as "reasonable" and "normal" to use Third World people and natural resources for their own financial benefit, at whatever cost to the indigenous peoples and the health of their lands.

The connections among the various forms of oppression are increasingly becoming clear to many, as evidenced by the World Council of Churches' inclusion of "the integrity of creation" in its rallying cry of "peace and justice." In the closing years of the 20th century we are being called to do something unprecedented: to think wholistically, to think about "everything that is," because everything on this planet is interrelated and interdependent and hence the fate of each is tied to the fate of the whole.

This state of affairs brought about a major "conversion" in my own theological journey. I began as a Barthian in the '50s, finding Barth's heady divine transcendence and "otherness" to be as invigorating as cold mountain air to my conventional religious upbringing. Like many of my generation, I found in Barth what appeared to be a refreshing and needed alternative to liberalism. But after years of work on the poetic, metaphorical nature of religious language (and hence its relative, constructive and necessarily changing character), and in view of feminism's critique of the hierarchical, dualistic nature of the language of the Jewish and Christian traditions, my bonds to biblicism and the Barthian God loosened. Those years were the "deconstructive" phase of my development as a theologian.

My constructive phase began upon reading Gordon Kaufman's 1983 Presidential Address to the American Academy of Religion. Kaufman called for a paradigm shift, given the exigencies of our time — the possibility of nuclear war. He called theologians to deconstruct and reconstruct the basic symbols of the Jewish and Christian traditions — God, Christ and Torah — so as to be on the side of life rather than against it, as was the central symbol of God with its traditional patriarchal, hierarchical, militaristic imagery. I answered this call, and my subsequent work has been concerned with contributing to that task.

While the nuclear threat has lessened somewhat, the threat of ecological deterioration has increased: they are related as "quick kill" to "slow death." In other words, we have been given some time. We need to use it well, for we may not have much of it. The agenda this shift sets for theologians is multifaceted, given the many different tasks that need to be done. This paradigm shift, if accepted, suggests a new mode of theological production, one characterized by advocacy, collegiality and the appreciation of differences.

Until the rise of liberation theologies, theology was more concerned with having intellectual respectability in the academy than with forging an alliance with the oppressed or particular political or social attitudes and practices. There was a convenient division between theology (concerned with the knowledge of God) and ethics (a lesser enterprise for action-oriented types). Theologians were also usually "solo" players, each concerned to write his (the "hers" were in short supply) magnum opus, a complete systematic theology. As the deconstructionists have underscored, these theologians also strove to assert, against different voices, the *one* voice (their own — or at least the voice of their own kind) as the truth, the "universal" truth.

Our situation calls for a different way of conducting ourselves as theologians. Like all people we need, in both our personal and professional lives, to work for the well-being of our planet and all its creatures. We need to work in a collegial fashion, realizing that we contribute only a tiny fragment. Feminists have often suggested a "quilt" metaphor as an appropriate methodology: each of us can contribute only a small "square" to the whole. Such a view of scholarship may appear alien to an academy that rewards works "totalizing" others in the field and insisting on one view.

The times are too perilous and it is too late in the day for such games. We need to work together, each in his or her own small way, to create a planetary situation that is more viable and less vulnerable. A collegial theology explicitly supports difference. One of the principal insights of both feminism and postmodern science is that while everything is interrelated and interdependent, everything (maple leaves, stars, deer, dirt — and not just human beings) is different from everything else. Individuality and interrelatedness are features of the universe; hence, no one voice or single species is the only one that counts.

While I realize that the focus for this series is on how one's mind has changed, the way mine has changed demands that I focus not on mapping my individual journey but on specifying how our minds ought to change, both now and in the future. If advocacy, collegiality and difference characterized theological reflection and if the agenda of theology widened to include the context of our planet, some significant changes would occur. I will suggest three.

First, it would mean a more or less common agenda for theological reflection, though one with an almost infinite number of different tasks. The encompassing agenda would be to deconstruct and reconstruct the central symbols of the Jewish and Christian traditions in favor of life and its fulfillment, keeping the liberation of the oppressed, including the earth and all its creatures, in central focus. That is so broad, so inclusive an agenda that it allows for myriad ways to construe it and carry it out. It does, however, turn the eyes of theologians away from heaven and toward the earth; or, more accurately, it causes us to connect the starry heavens with the earth, as the "common" creation story claims, telling us that everything in the universe, including stars, dirt, robins, black holes, sunsets, plants and human beings, is the product of an enormous explosion billions of years ago. In whatever ways we might reconstruct the symbols of God, human being and earth, this can no longer be done in a dualistic fashion, for the heavens and the earth are one phenomenon, albeit an incredibly ancient, rich and varied one.

If theology is going to reflect wholistically, that is, in terms of the picture of current reality, then it must do so in ways consonant with the new story of creation. One clear directive that this story gives theology is to understand human beings as earthlings (not aliens or tourists on the planet) and God as immanently present in the processes of the universe, including those of our planet. Such a focus has important implications for the contribution of theologians to "saving the planet," for theologies emerging from a coming together of God and humans *in and on the earth* implies a cosmocentric rather than anthropocentric focus. This does not, by the way, mean that theology should reject theocentrism; rather, it means that the divine concern includes *all* of creation. Nor does it imply the substitution of a creation focus for the tradition's concern with redemption; rather, it insists that redemption should include all dimensions of creation, not just human beings.

A second implication of accepting this paradigm shift is a focus on praxis. As Juan Segundo has said, theology is not one of the "liberal arts," for it contains an element of the prophetic, making it at the very least an unpopular enterprise and at times a dangerous one. The academy has been suspicious of it with good reason, willing to accept religious studies but aware that theology contains an element of commitment foreign to the canons of scholarly objectivity. (Marxist or Freudian commitments, curiously, have been acceptable in the academy, but not theological ones.) Increasingly, however, the hermeneutics of suspicion and deconstruction are helping to unmask simplistic, absolutist notions of objectivity, revealing a variety of perspectives, interpretations, commitments and contexts. Moreover, this variety is being viewed as not only enriching but necessary. Hence the emphasis on praxis and commitment, on a concerned theology, need in no way imply a lack of scholarly rigor or a retreat to fideism. Rather, it insists that one of the criteria of constructive theological reflection — thinking about our place in the earth and the earth's relation to its source — is a concern with the *consequences* of proposed constructions for those who live within them.

Theological constructs are no more benign than scientific ones. With the marriage of science and technology beginning in the 17th century, the commitments and concerns of the scientific community have increasingly been determined by the military-industrial-government complex that funds basic research. The ethical consequences of scientific research — which projects get funded and the consequences of the funded projects — are or ought to be *scientific* issues and not issues merely for the victims of the fall-out of these projects. Likewise, theological reflection is a *concerned* affair, concerned that this constructive thinking be on the side of the well-being of the planet and all its creatures. For centuries people have lived within the constructs of Christian reflection and interpretation, unknowingly as well as knowingly. Some of these constructs have been liberating, but many others have been oppressive, patriarchal and provincial. Indeed, theology is not a "liberal art," but a prophetic activity, announcing and interpreting the salvific love of God to all of creation.

A third implication of this paradigm shift is that the theological task is not only diverse in itself (there are many theologies), but also contributes to the planetary agenda of the 21st century, an agenda that beckons and challenges us to move beyond nationalism, militarism, limitless economic growth, consumerism, uncontrollable population growth and ecological

141

deterioration. In ways that have never before been so clear and stark, we have met the enemy and know it is ourselves. While the wholistic, planetary perspective leads some to insist that all will be well if a "creation spirituality" were to replace the traditional "redemption spirituality" of the Christian tradition, the issue is not that simple. It is surely the case that the overemphasis on redemption to the neglect of creation needs to be redressed; moreover, there is much in the common creation story that calls us to a profound appreciation of the wonders of our being and the being of all other creatures. Nonetheless, it is doubtful that such knowledge and appreciation will be sufficient to deal with the exigencies of our situation.

The enemy — indifferent, selfish, shortsighted, xenophobic, anthropocentric, greedy human beings — calls, at the very least, for a renewed emphasis on sin as the cause of much of the planet's woes and an emphasis on a broad and profound repentance. Theology, along with other institutions, fields of study and expertise, can deepen our sense of complicity in the earth's decay. In addition to turning our eyes and hearts to an appreciation of the beauty, richness and singularity of our planet through a renewed theology of creation and nature, theology ought also to underscore and elaborate on the myriad ways that we personally and corporately have ruined and continue to ruin God's splendid creation — acts which we and no other creature can knowingly commit. The present dire situation calls for radicalizing the Christian understanding of sin and evil. Human responsibility for the fate of the earth is a recent and terrible knowledge; our loss of innocence is total, for we know what we have done. If theologians were to accept this context and agenda of their work, they would see themselves in dialogue with all those in other areas and fields similarly engaged: those who feed the homeless and fight for animal rights; the cosmologists who tell us of the common origins (and hence interrelatedness) of all forms of matter and life; economists who examine how we must change if the earth is to support its population; the legislators and judges who work to advance civil rights for those discriminated against in our society; the Greenham women who picket nuclear plants; and the women of northern India who literally "hug" trees to protect them from destruction, and so on and on.

Theology is an "earthly" affair in the best sense of that word: it helps people to live rightly, appropriately, on the earth, in our home. It is, as the Jewish and Christian traditions have always insisted, concerned with "right relations," relations with God, neighbor and self, but now the context has broadened to include what has dropped out of the picture in the past few hundred years — the oppressed neighbors, the other creatures and the earth that supports us all. This shift could be seen as a return to the roots of a tradition that has insisted on the creator, redeemer God as the source and salvation of all that is. We now know that "all that is" is vaster, more complex, more awesome, more interdependent, than any other people has ever known. The new theologies that emerge from such a context have the opportunity to view divine transcendence in deeper, more awesome and more intimate ways than ever before. They also have the obligation to understand human beings and all other forms of life as radically interrelated and interdependent as well as to understand our special responsibility for the planet's well-being.

My own work takes place within this context and attempts to add a small square to the growing planetary quilt.

Eberhard Jüngel

Toward the Heart of the Matter

Have I changed? I hope so. Changelessness *(immutabilitas)* would not be a compliment even for God, and the old metaphysics was badly advised when it thought it had to pay this compliment to the divine being. No historical being — and the God who has come into the world in Jesus of Nazareth has, no less than a human creature, a history — can become himself or herself without changing. The less fundamental question remains, therefore, How have I changed? On that score good friends and perhaps even candid opponents could give a more precise account than I. After all, who knows him- or herself? I know myself rather poorly, and I of all people am especially eager to learn exactly — at least on that good old Judgment Day — "how my mind has changed."

There is, however, a series of unforgettable situations, encounters and experiences that has perceptibly influenced and molded me and without which — if I am not completely deceived — I would not be the person I am today. I shall restrict myself here to my "theological existence." It is, to be sure, virtually identical with my daily life. But even in the life of a

Eberhard Jüngel is professor of systematic theology and philosophy at the University of Tübingen.

theologian there is more than what is of public interest. For example, that I have become over the course of time a more or less adequate cook has an explicitly political cause. That fact, however, is unlikely to interest even my guests, provided they don't have to suffer any bad results of my culinary skills. The view, which is gaining more and more currency even in Europe, that everything in the life of a human being is of general interest and, for that reason, is open to public reporting I take to be a dangerous misperception (presumably originating in Calvinism) of the personal dignity of the human being, who is more than what deserves to be published about him or her. *Individuum est ineffabile.* Thank God.

The event or, more exactly, the chain of events which has moved me more than anything else recently is the collapse of "realized socialism" in the countries of the former East bloc, including my own homeland. I happened to be in the U.S. (for the first time, by the way) when the great 1989 demonstrations in Leipzig took place which finally brought about that "gentle revolution," as a consequence of which the partition of Germany has now come to an end. The careful reporting of the exciting events in distant Europe by the American media and the lively interest of my colleagues there certainly contributed to the fact that, in the middle of Texas and then in Chicago and New York, the time of the building of the Berlin Wall and the even more distant time of my youth in Magdeburg began to speak to me in a new way. I became aware how deeply experiences long ago had left their mark upon me. And so, considerably more than is usually the case in this series, I must return to my beginnings as I attempt to review my theological existence in its identity and in its changes.

In my parental home religion was not discussed, and my desire to study theology met with the concerned astonishment of my mother and the resolute refusal of my father. To be sure, my mother had taught her children to pray, but she feared that the choice of the pastoral vocation would not exactly open up bright prospects for the future in the socialist society of the

German Democratic Republic. We lived in Magdeburg on the Elbe, which even though it was conquered by the American troops in 1945 was handed over to the Red Army camped on the other side of the river. And my father had nothing but ridicule for the Christian faith. That I nevertheless held fast to my intention and finally even realized it certainly cannot be explained merely as the adolescent rebellion of a son against his father's authority.

There was, however, one experience that affected me even more deeply than had my experiences at home, and which was decisive for my choice. It continues to shape me even now. That was the discovery of the church as the one place within a Stalinist society where one could speak the truth without being penalized. What a liberating experience in the face of the ideological-political pressure that dominated in school! Friends were arrested, I myself was interrogated more than once — only because we dared to say what we thought. Immediately before the Workers' Revolt in 1953 I was denounced, together with other young Christians, as an "enemy of the republic" and expelled from school before a full assembly of teachers and students expressly convened on the day before the university entrance exams. Our fellow students were ordered to break off all contact with us. As I left the hall named after the Humboldt brothers — but dominated by a completely different spirit! — the upright among my teachers turned away in helpless silence. It was a scene pregnant with symbolism, in which the truth of the Ciceronian maxim (a maxim that had been pounded into us by the very same teachers) suddenly dawned on me: *cum tacent, clamant* ("when they are silent they cry loudest"). In the Christian church, however, one was free to break through the silence and the pressure to lie that was growing stronger all the time. Here one dared to bear witness to the truth of the gospel in such a way that its liberating power could also be experienced in very worldly, very political terms.

If one begins to analyze why "realized socialism" finally failed — now that the entire system has collapsed like a house of cards — one should seek the decisive cause in its *objective untruthfulness*. Although far from espousing antisocialism in principle, I nevertheless cannot shut my eyes to the untruthful way in which the socialist ideals were implemented by a kind of power politics. One can argue about the ideals of socialism. But that also entails the possibility of arguing against them. And precisely this was not allowed.

Hand in hand with the ideological control of thought was a corresponding distrust of every deviation from Marxist dogma and its official interpretation by the Central Committee of the party: a total distrust that necessarily brought about the totalitarian surveillance state. Its hallmark did not consist chiefly in the fact that the dominant political class deceived itself along with the oppressed citizens. Rather, the monopoly on truth claimed by the Communist Party and implemented by governmental force was directed against truth itself, as is every claim to truth implemented by violence. It produced a perversion of thinking to which even the perpetrators had to fall victim. The pressure to deceive oneself along with the public dominated all aspects of the society, even economic decisions. Therefore, it must have been tantamount to a revolution when Mikhail Gorbachev began to demand *glasnost*. His courage to look reality in the face and to break the ideological taboos remains an act of political greatness, even if — God forbid — his politics of *perestroika* should, in the final analysis, fail.

What does all that have to do with my theological thinking? At least this much is clear: on the basis of these experiences in which I encountered the church as an institution of truth and, for that reason, as an institution of freedom, I decided to become (my father's veto notwithstanding) a theologian, and to this day I have not seriously regretted that decision. When my dear colleagues Johann Baptist Metz and Jürgen Moltmann later initiated the project of a "political theology" and developed it with great impact, I insisted on the basis of those experiences that the political relevance of Christian faith consists, from beginning to end, in its ability and obligation to speak the truth.

The political activity required of the church aims, above all else, to assist the cause of truth.

At first I pursued more far-reaching proposals in the European context with a certain restraint, because I feared a renewed political interdict (a clericalization of society from the left, so to speak) in any program that would bind all Christians theologically to a particular political course or even elevate "revolution" to a theological principle. On the other hand, the adherents of "political theology" appeared, in my eyes, to be much too abstract when it came to the concrete situations of life. They seemed to feign concreteness by all kinds of activism. At any rate, that's how the issue looked to me at first, at least in the European context. But the significance that "liberation theology" assumed, both in the context of the scandalous social injustice of the so-called Third World and in the context of South African racism, taught me better. The immeasurable shame that I felt as a white person in South African townships has completely persuaded me that the Christian is permitted, indeed commanded, to work against an unjust system, not only with thoughts and words but even with deeds. To be sure, the person of faith must assume *individual responsibility* for that decision. And in no instance should anyone be coerced theologically to take up violence.

To this day it irritates me that in this regard something like a liberation theology for the oppressed people in the world of "realized socialism" was apparently never considered. Even in the headquarters of the World Council of Churches on the Genevan route de Ferney, where injustice in other parts of the world was so courageously identified by name and resistance movements were energetically supported, one feigned blindness to the conditions in Romania, for example, right up until the end. That is an ecumenical scandal. And one can only hope that this dark shadow will not darken the undeniable achievements of ecumenism.

However much the political realization of Marxism-Leninism in the "socialist brother nations" failed to impress me

148

positively, still the atheism to which Marxist theory and its adherents are committed posed a challenge that continues to engage me. It should give one pause to consider that people in the GDR apparently allowed themselves to be more impressed with the atheistic option of Marxism than with its political and economic form. At any rate, the great number of Germans living on the other side of the Elbe who don't belong to any religious community speaks for itself. The encounter with atheism, quite apart from all statistics, has consistently stimulated my thought since the beginning of my teaching career.

Apropos my teaching career: I became a theological teacher literally overnight on account of the building of the Berlin Wall. When Erich Honecker, under orders from Walter Ulbricht, raised the wall, thereby cementing the division of Germany, the seminary students who lived in East Berlin were cut off from their professors who lived in West Berlin. In order to ease the academic emergency, Kurt Scharf, who would later become the bishop of Berlin, appointed me to a teaching position. Just a few weeks before I had received my doctorate in theology. (A few months later police headquarters in East Berlin wanted to take the doctorate away from me.) As a consequence, I was very poorly prepared. Thus I began to burn a lot of midnight oil. Often on the evening before I still didn't know what I would lecture on the next morning (yes, academic nights are long).

The theology that emerged in this fashion would today perhaps be called "contextual." It was contextual insofar as I asked myself how the language about God that the biblical texts empower us to speak can demonstrate its truth in a situation shaped by atheism. It seemed to me too cheap simply to demonize atheism or to unmask it as a pseudo-religion. I felt myself obligated, rather, to understand atheism better than it understands itself, and I tried to go into the heart of the matter. It soon became crystal clear to me that what manifested itself in the Eastern bloc in an extremely intolerant way completely determines the modern and postmodern world in a much more subtle way. Upon closer inspection I realized that not even religion and atheism must be mutually exclusive — a paradox. The atheistic character of the age seems, therefore, to be something different from the "religionlessness" foretold by Dietrich Bonhoeffer. Had not Schleiermacher already commented that "a religion without God can be better than one with God"?

The newly awakened religiosity of the past few years — in Europe it has to do largely with a vagabond form of religion — should not, therefore, be celebrated by a hasty apologetics as the overcoming of atheism. On the contrary, I have been and continue to be concerned with discovering a moment of truth in atheism, a moment which is at least as important as that to be found in a theistic metaphysics. Is it merely an accident that the young Christian movement was charged with atheism in its religious environment? Did not the radical negation of the ancient world of gods by the Old Testament prophets and by the Word of the crucified Son of God prepare the ground upon which modern atheism could thrive? Did not Nietzsche recognize, more clearly than many theologians, that the proclamation of the crucified God threatened to become a negation of Deity? The answer to this question is certainly not to be found in the "death-of-God theology" that aroused some interest in the U.S. a quarter of a century ago. But the fact that the expression "death of God" has a Christian origin should give us something to think about. I have thought about it, and I can conceive of the God who overcomes death only in such a way that God himself is nothing other than the unity of life and death on behalf of life. As such he bears the marks of our godlessness within himself: a godlessness the overcoming of which was and is his concern, not ours.

It goes without saying that I resolutely reject any old-style or new-style theological apologetics that denounces atheism as a deficient mode of human existence. What gives us the right to suppose that the atheist is less a human person than the pious Jew or Christian? On the basis of such religious propaganda the proclamation of the justification of the godless can hardly flourish. Whoever wishes to advocate the overcoming of godlessness through God would do much better to take the atheist seriously as a particularly mature specimen of *homo humanus*.

In my efforts not only to understand the truth of the gospel but also to assume personal responsibility for teaching it, it proved to be an invaluable aid that a friendly providence placed noteworthy teachers of very different orientations in the student's path. As I began to study Kant intensively with Gerhard Stammler and as I familiarized myself with both classical logic and symbolic logic, warnings were being issued about the philosophy of Martin Heidegger. At the same time, however, I was being exhorted to study the texts of Heidegger by the New Testament scholar Ernst Fuchs, who put me in touch with his teacher Rudolf Bultmann. In an "illegal" semester spent outside of the GDR — moving back and forth between Zürich, Basel and Freiburg — I finally heard the master himself. At the time, Heidegger was "on the way to language" *(unterwegs zur Sprache)*.

Toward the end of his life I had a conversation with Heidegger about the relation between thought and language, and I asked whether it wasn't the destiny of thought to be on the way to God *(unterwegs zu Gott)*. He answered: "God — that is the most worthy object of thought. But that's where language breaks down."

Admittedly, this was not the impression I had received during that memorable semester. At the time, Gerhard Ebeling in Zürich had introduced me to the thought of Martin Luther, while Karl Barth in Basel was making me familiar with his own thought. Barth's theology, flowing like a broad stream and suffering from an excess of argumentation, didn't exactly give the impression of a language breaking down. At first Barth looked upon me as a sort of spy from the Bultmann school and greeted me with unconcealed skepticism. But when I dared, in an unforgettable meeting of his group, not only to contradict the Basel criticism of Bultmann with a vehemence born of youthful audacity but also proceeded to interpret one section from Barth's anthropology to his satisfaction, I was invited for a late-night dispute over a bottle of wine. And a few days later the entire *Church Dogmatics* stood in front of my door with the dedication: "To Eberhard Jüngel, on the way into God's beloved eastern zone."

A few years later, when I myself had to offer lectures and seminars in dogmatics and was looking around for some helpful guidance, I immersed myself again in this magnum opus of my teacher. And behold, in the midst of a theological discussion that was increasingly losing all perspective I saw that I had encountered in Barth the thought of someone who truly believed in his subject matter. Barth's theology was autochthonous. From it one could learn that substantive concentration upon the truth to which the Bible bears witness is the best prerequisite for keeping faith in the present world. I gained a new acquaintance with the tradition, in relation to which there was neither a disrespectful criticism nor an uncritical respect. Thereby an ecumenical horizon opened up for me, without which I simply cannot conceive any future theology.

Above all, I was challenged to think about God from the event of his revelation, and that means from the event of his coming into the world: hence, as a God to whom nothing human is foreign and who, in the person of Jesus Christ, has come nearer to humanity than humanity is able to come near to itself. The Augustinian *interior intimo meo* ("nearer than I am to myself") became something of a hermeneutical key, not only for the correct understanding of God but also for the correct understanding of the human being, whose subjective godlessness is mercifully anticipated by God's objective humanity. In short, in contrast to the sterile Barth-scholasticism that dominated Germany at the time and that had built around the master's dogmatics a Chinese "Great Wall" not to be penetrated, in my case something like a "new frontiers" mentality grew out of my encounter with the person and work of Karl Barth.

It is no wonder, then, that it never occurred to me to settle down in the so-called Barth school. Nor in the Bultmann school either, for that matter. It didn't even occur to me to suppose that the Reformers always had the deeper insight and the most adequate solution to all theological problems. I say this with all due respect for the unusually incisive theology of the Reformers, which has not even yet come to the end of its historical influence. But the truth of theology is richer than that of its schools of thought. That is why to this very day I have steadfastly refused to succumb to the temptation to make disciples of my own. To be sure, students are undoubtedly eager for that sort of thing; and not a few of my listeners have pressured me to orchestrate something like a theological school.

But, according to the measure of my insight, a theological teacher can have "disciples" only in the sense that he teaches them to immerse themselves more thoroughly in the lifelong school of Holy Scripture, in order that there they may find the criteria for the training of their own faculty of judgment. The pastor, by the way, has an analogous task with respect to the congregation. Evangelical (i.e., Protestant) theology is at least in this respect the heir (perhaps even the mother?) of the Enlightenment, because it gives us the courage to use our own understanding as it has been trained by the hearing of God's Word. Only in this way is the consensus of believers in a common confession before God and before the world worth anything at all. In this sense theology must, I am convinced, pursue enlightenment in the light of the gospel — beyond neo-orthodoxy and neorationalism, but also beyond collectivism and individualism. In this way I have tried since 1961 to make theology both appetizing and obligatory to the students entrusted to me: as a *theologia viatorum,* a "theology of pilgrims," who are "on the way to the heart of the matter" *(unterwegs zur Sache)* and who must always keep widening the boundaries of their insight. "New frontiers . . ."

When I finally moved from East Berlin to Zürich and then to Tübingen, it was a step forward into new territory — in a quite different sense, but no less momentous. I vacillated for a long time over whether to accept the invitation of a Swiss university and to leave "realized socialism" for the ostensibly capitalist world of the West. In the end, two conversations, one with Johannes Jänicke, bishop of Magdeburg, and the other with Barth, played a crucial role in my decision. Quite independently of one another, they both gave me the same advice for the same reason: in Zürich I would be free of the fixation on the "dictatorship of the proletariat" that was unavoidable in the GDR and the corresponding danger of intellectual paralysis.

In fact, as I sought to orient myself in the colorful, sometimes too colorful, Western world, I noticed how in every respect life behind the iron curtain was in danger of becoming one-dimensional. In body and soul and with every fiber of my being I felt the dreary grayness of that walled-in world beginning to fall away from me. The intense love of truth that had hitherto determined my theological existence was now matched by a passionate love of life.

Perhaps that's the reason why faith in the Creator has increasingly occupied my theological attention. Previously the powerlessness of the crucified one had claimed my thought and challenged me to conceive of the doctrine of God, as much as possible, apart from metaphysics. Now, however, my concern was learning to think about the creative omnipotence in such a way that it proves itself to be divine power precisely in its capacity for powerlessness (even to the point of death on a cross). In direct contrast to the sweeping denunciation of the concepts power, dominion, achievement, etc., which is growing stronger in the Christian churches, it seems to me, rather, that theological clarification of these terms is called for. Neither the being of the Creator nor that of his creation is even conceivable apart from the exercise of dominion and power. I was provoked by the peace movement and the ecological crisis not to forgo the denounced terms but to determine their correct use.

In this regard the impetus my thought had received from Heidegger proved helpful. It became clear to me that the exercise of dominion and power ought not to be for imperial designs of one's own but must be understood as *Dominium* for the benefit of what exists, for the "saving of the phenomena."

Therefore, dominion is only legitimate as dominion over oneself. That holds true not only in the interpersonal realm but also in relation to the nonhuman creation. The mandate *Dominium terrae* given to the human being by the Creator (Gen. 1:26f.) is not obsolete, but its misuse is. Long before it had become fashionable, Heidegger had exposed the metaphysical origins of this misuse. His own "thought about being" *(Seinsdenken)* already implied something like an ecology at a time when people who would later become ecologists ridiculed him for being a romantic.

My encounter with this thinker, however, has proven to be of enduring significance in many respects, not least of which is that it prevented me from an anthropomonism in the doctrine of creation. I made a mental note of his statement: "Philosophy perishes when it has become anthropology." *Mutatis mutandis,* the same holds true for theology. We human beings must learn to understand ourselves as relational beings instead of as subjects in the center of things. We must learn to conceive of being as a *being-together* instead of as substance. Then and only then will the usurped *Imperium* become once again the *Dominium terrae* that the Creator entrusted to his creation.

The recognition of the perversion of the *Dominium terrae* into an anthropomonistic *Imperium,* visible in the contemporary crises that have been precipitated by the misuse of scientific knowledge, has made me newly aware of a philosophical and theological deficiency: we lack a gradation of evil. I stumbled onto this for the first time as a result of the attempts — which, to be sure, have hitherto failed — to locate the place of theology "after Auschwitz," and then again in the face of the political terrorism and the "terror of virtue" that became apparent in it. Even the Christian doctrine of sin seemed to me to be deficient, either in spite of or on account of every imaginable scholasticism regarding sin. It is high time that we expose the common reduction of evil to a mere infringement of the moral law as a trivialization from which evil profits. A gradation of evil, yet to be developed, must certainly proceed from this insight which, to be sure, is given only on the basis of the experience of reconciliation: anything that renders problematic being as a being-together deserves to be called evil. The tendency toward a lack of rationality, beginning in a misuse of the relational richness of life, finds its terrible consummation in death's perfect lack of relationality.

As a countermove, so to speak, to the demand for a gradation of evil, my interest has for some time been directed toward eschatology, which I interpret as the definitive being-together of the Creator with his creation and of the creatures with one another. Is there anything like that, at least in a preliminary way, before the last day? Can we implement in the world earthly analogies to the kingdom of God, at least in a fragmentary way? The answer to this question affects not only my concept of a political ethic but also considerations for a theology of the religions, the necessity of which Wolfhart Pannenberg and Hans Küng have vividly set before me. How can the being-together of the religions succeed when the Christian faith insists that Jesus Christ is the salvation of all people? Can theology and the church disavow that without losing their identity? I admire those of my colleagues who frankly admit that in this respect they have crossed the Rubicon and bid a resolute farewell to *Solus Christus* as an intolerant claim to absoluteness. But I fear that they have confused the Rubicon with the Halys . . .

Nonetheless, it remains an urgent task to travel the road toward a theology of the religions — which would have to include atheism among its concerns — in such a way that the christological *particula exclusiva* would not be misused in order to make a claim for the absoluteness of Christianity. The trinitarian being of God, which I understand as a *community of mutual otherness,* could be an incentive to develop models of earthly being-together: *vestigia trinitatis,* as it were, in which creatures would be enabled to exist in communities of mutual otherness (this could also be relevant for political ethics). To be sure, the kingdom of God wouldn't thereby be brought about. But in spite of that, the earth would be protected from becoming hell.

In a very concrete way I have been presented with the task and the opportunity to help build an earthly community of mutual otherness. Beginning this winter semester I will be a guest professor at Martin Luther University in Halle-Wittenberg, in addition to keeping my teaching responsibilities in Tübingen (to which belongs, by the way, the office of the dean of the Tübingen Stift, where once Hegel, Schelling, Hölderlin and other magnificent minds went to school). This will not simply be a return home — although it touches me in a homey sort of way that among those who learned something in my classes in Berlin are a few who are counted among the new politicians of the GDR, specifically among the realists *(Realpolitiker)*. Indeed, there waits for me in Halle a new generation. And working together with students who have been raised very differently in what was formerly the GDR certainly poses once again a new frontier in my theological existence. I anticipate that this will be one of the most beautiful redrawings of a border.

July 15, 1990
(Translated by Paul E. Capetz)

Jon Sobrino

Awakening from the Sleep of Inhumanity

I have been asked to write about "how my mind has changed," and I must say that it has changed indeed — though not just my mind, I hope, but my will and heart as well. Because the changes that I have experienced and will write about have also been experienced by many others in El Salvador and throughout Latin America, I will be using singular and plural pronouns interchangeably.

I am writing for the North American reader, who, almost by definition, has difficulty understanding the Latin American reality and the deep changes which that reality can bring about. I will therefore try to explain the essence of such fundamental change from the perspective of El Salvador, comparing it with another change which is often said to lie at the heart of so-called modern Western civilization. From the time of Kant such change has been described as an awakening from a "dogmatic slumber" — an awakening that is like the liberation of reason from subjection to authority and which, in turn, gives rise to

---

Jon Sobrino, S.J., is a member of the faculty of José Simeón Cañas Central American University in San Salvador.

the dogmatic proclamation that the fundamental liberation of the human being lies in the liberation of reason.

In the Third World, the fundamental change also consists of an awakening, but from another type of sleep, or better, from a nightmare — the sleep of inhumanity. It is the awakening to the reality of an oppressed and subjugated world, a world whose liberation is the basic task of every human being so that in this way human beings may finally come to be human.

Such is the change that has occurred in me and in many others. And what has brought about such a profound and un-expected change is encounter with the reality of the poor and the victims of this world. In order to put all this in simple terms, permit me to offer a bit of biographical background prior to more deliberate reflection.

I was born in 1938 in Spain's Basque region, where I grew up. In 1957 I came to El Salvador as a novice in the Society of Jesus, and since then I have lived in this country, with two notable interruptions: five years in St. Louis studying philoso-phy and engineering, and seven years in Frankfurt studying theology. So I know fairly well both the world of development and abundance and the world of poverty and death.

I must confess that until 1974 when I returned to El Salvador, the world of the poor — that is, the real world — did not exist for me. When I arrived in El Salvador in 1957 I witnessed appalling poverty, but even though I saw it with my eyes, I did not really see it; thus that poverty had nothing to say to me for my own life as a young Jesuit and as a human being. It did not even cross my mind that I might learn something from the poor. Everything which was important for my life as a Jesuit I brought with me from Europe — and if anything had to change, that would come from Europe as well. My vision of my task as a priest was a traditional one: I would help the Salvadorans to replace their popular "super-stitious" religiosity with a more sophisticated kind, and I would help the Latin American branches of the church (the European church) to grow. I was the typical "missionary," full of good will and Eurocentricity — and blind to reality.

Further studies in philosophy and theology induced a rude awakening from "dogmatic slumber." During those years of study I and my fellow students went through Kant and Hegel, through Marx and Sartre, and engaged in serious questioning at every stage. To put it bluntly, we began questioning the God we had inherited from our pious Central American, Spanish and Basque families. We delved into exegetical criticism and Bultmann's demythologizing, into the legacy of modernism and the relativism of the church — all of which took one logically to a profound questioning not only of what we had been taught by the church, but also of the Christ himself.

We had to awaken from the dream. Painful and wrenching in my case, it was as if layers of skin were being removed one by one. Fortunately, there was light as well as darkness in the awakening. Karl Rahner's theology — I mention him because he was for me the one who left the most lasting and beneficial impression — was my companion during those years, and his pages on the mystery of God continue to accompany me even today. Vatican II gave us new insights and new enthusiasm; it helped us realize that the church is not itself the most important thing, not even for God. In working on my doctoral thesis on Christology I began again to discover Jesus of Nazareth. He was not the abstract Christ I had imagined before, nor was he the Christ being presented by Pierre Teilhard de Chardin as "the final point of all evolution," nor by Rahner as "the absolute bearer of all salvation." I discovered that the Christ is none other than Jesus and that he conceived a utopia on which all too few have focused: the ideal of the kingdom of God.

The churchly triumphalism of our youth was far behind us now. We considered ourselves avant-garde and "progressive," even thinking ourselves well prepared to set the Salvadoran people on the right track. Nevertheless, even with many changes for the better we had not changed fundamentally. I, at least, continued to be a First World product, and if I were changing, it was in accordance with that First World's process at that world's pace and by that world's laws. Although it was a necessary change in many ways, it was insufficiently radical and, from a Third World point of view, it was superficial. For me the world continued to be the "First World," the church continued to be the European church of Vatican II, theology continued to be German theology, and utopia continued to mean that in some way the countries of the south would become like those of the north. That was what many of us wanted, consciously or not, to work for at that time. We had awakened from the dogmatic slumber, if you will, but we continued to sleep in the much deeper sleep of inhumanity — the sleep of egocentrism and selfishness. But eventually we did wake up.

Through one of those strange miracles which happen in history I came to realize that while I had both acquired much knowledge and gotten rid of much traditional baggage, deep down nothing had changed. I saw that my life and studies had not given me new eyes to see this world as it really is, and that they hadn't taken from me the heart of stone I had for the suffering of this world.

That realization is what I experimented upon after returning to El Salvador in 1974. And I began, I believe, to awaken from the sleep of inhumanity. To my surprise, I found that some of my fellow Jesuits had already begun to speak of the poor and of injustice and of liberation. I also found that some Jesuits, priests, religious, farmers and students, even some bishops, were acting on behalf of the poor and getting into serious difficulties as a consequence. Having just arrived, I didn't know what possible contribution I might make. But from the beginning it became quite clear that truth, love, faith, the gospel of Jesus, God, the very best we have as people of faith and as human beings — these were somehow to be found among the poor and in the cause of justice. I do not mean to imply that Rahner and Jürgen Moltmann, whom I studied avidly, no longer had anything to say to me. But I did come to understand that it was absurd to go about trying to Rahnerize or Moltmannize the people of El Salvador. If there was something positive I could bring from the perspective of my studies, the task would have to be the reverse: if at all possible, we needed to Salvadorize Rahner and Moltmann.

At this point I was fortunate enough to find others who had already awakened from the sleep of inhumanity, among them Ignacio Ellacuría and Archbishop Oscar Romero, to name just two great Salvadoran Christians, martyrs and friends. But beyond those happy encounters, little by little I came face to face with the truly poor, and I am convinced that they were the ones who brought about the final awakening. Once awakened, my questions and especially my answers to questions became radically different. The basic question came to be: Are we really human and, if we are believers, is our faith human? The reply was not the anguish which follows an awakening from dogmatic sleep, but the joy which comes when we are willing not only to change the mind from enslavement to liberation, but also to change our vision in order to see what had been there, unnoticed, all along, and to change hearts of stone into hearts of flesh — in other words, to let ourselves be moved to compassion and mercy.

The jigsaw puzzle of human life, whose pattern had broken apart as we went through a period of analysis and questioning, again broke apart when we met the poor of this world. But there was a significant difference. Following the awakening from dogmatic sleep, we had the hard task of piecing the puzzle together again, and we obtained some rather positive results. But such a first awakening was not enough to shake us from ourselves. Wakening from the sleep of inhumanity was a stronger jolt but a more joyous one. It is possible to live an intellectually honest life in this world, but it is also possible to live sensitively and joyfully. And then I realized another long-forgotten fact: that the gospel is not just truth — which must be reconciled in the light of all our questioning — but is, above all, good news which produces joy.

In reflecting on this questioning and this joyful change, I would like to zero in on what is most important: the new eyes we receive when we awaken from the sleep of inhumanity to the reality of what is fundamental.

For the past 17 years in El Salvador I have had to witness many things: the darkness of poverty and injustice, of numerous and frightful massacres, but also the luminosity of hope and the endless generosity of the poor. What I want to stress, however, is the discovery which precedes all this: the revelation of the truth of reality and, through it, the truth of human beings and of God.

In El Salvador a phrase of Paul's in his Letter to the Romans was driven home to me: "The wrath of God is revealed from heaven against all ungodliness and wickedness of men who by their wickedness suppress the truth" (Rom. 1:18). I began to understand that it is not enough to go beyond ignorance to truth, as we are often taught to believe; it is pointless to aspire to truth unless we are also willing to distill its consequences. From that moment I considered myself fortunate to have reality show forth its truth to me.

The first thing we discovered in El Salvador was that this world is one gigantic cross for millions of innocent people who die at the hands of executioners. Father Ellacuría referred to them as "entire crucified peoples." And that is the salient fact of our world — quantitatively because it encompasses two-thirds of humanity, and qualitatively because it is the most cruel and scandalous of realities.

To use plain Christian talk, we have come to identify our world by its proper name: sin. Now this is a reality which a lot of believers and nonbelievers alike in the First World do not know how to handle. We call it by that name because, Christianly speaking, sin is "that which deals death." Sin is what dealt death to the Son of God, and sin is what continues to deal death to the sons and daughters of God. One may or may not believe in God, but because of the reality of death no one will be able to deny the reality of sin.

From this basic reality of the cross and of death we have learned to place in its true perspective the massive poverty which draws people to death — death which is slow at the hands of the ever-present structures of injustice, and death which is swift and violent when the poor seek to change their lot. We are currently numbering 75,000 dead in El Salvador.

We have learned that the world's poor are practically of no consequence to anyone — not to the people who live in abundance nor to the people who have any kind of power. For that reason the poor may also be defined as those who have ranged against them all the powers of this world. They certainly have against them the oligarchies, the multinational corporations, the various armed forces and virtually every government. They are also of no great consequence to the political parties, the universities or even the churches. (There are notable exceptions, of course, such as Archbishop Romero's church and Father Ellacuría's university.) If the poor are of no consequence as individuals within their own countries, they are also of no consequence as entire peoples amid the nations of the world. The First World is not interested in the Third World, to put it mildly. As history shows, it is only interested in ways to despoil the Third World in order to increase its own abundance.

People do not want to acknowledge or face up to the reality of a crucified world, and even less do we want to ask ourselves what is our share of responsibility for such a world. The world of poverty truly is the great unknown. It is surprising that the First World can know so much and yet ignore what is so fundamental about the world in which we live. It is also frustrating, because the problem is not a lack of means by which to learn the truth. We have enough knowledge to place a man on the Moon or on Mars, but we sometimes do not even know how many human beings share this planet, much less how many of them die every year from hunger (the number must be around 30 million), or what is happening in Guatemala or in Chad, or how much destruction was caused in Iraq by the 80,000 bombing sorties of the so-called allies.

It isn't that we simply do not know; we do not want to know because, at least subconsciously, we sense that we have all had something to do with bringing about such a crucified world. And as usually happens where scandal is involved, we have organized a vast cover-up before which the scandals of Watergate, Irangate or Iraqgate pale in comparison.

To "wake from sleep" in El Salvador goes far beyond the endless discussions on secondary topics which go on within churches and parties, even progressive churches and parties. The important thing is to remember that such an awakening is made possible by the world of the poor and the victimized. And it requires a fresh reading of some basic scriptural passages.

In El Salvador we have rediscovered how God looks at God's crucified creation. To recall the anthropomorphic but eloquent words of Genesis: "The Lord saw that the wickedness of human-kind was great in the earth. And the Lord was sorry that he had made humankind on the earth, and it grieved him to his heart." To put this in even more anthropological terms, we do not know how it is possible to be a human being and have not felt at some time the shame of belonging to inhuman humanity. We have rediscovered many other passages from Scripture whose original power far exceeds any meaning uncovered by exegetical and criti-cal scholarship — passages such as "the darkness hated the light" and, even more radically, "the Evil One is an assassin and a liar."

This world of poverty and of crucified peoples is what has allowed us to overcome blindness and to discover mendacity. As Scripture says, in Yahweh's suffering servant there is a light and in the crucified Christ there is wisdom. If we are blessed enough to look closely at those peoples, we begin to see a little more of the truth of things. The discovery can be startling at first, but it is also blessed because in this way we are true to ourselves and because the truth of the poor is more than just suffering and death.

Indeed, the poor of this world continue to demonstrate that they have hope, something which is close to disappearing elsewhere, other than the hope generated by an optimistic belief in progress or by the possibility of life beyond death. And the latter is not at all what Christian faith postulates. What Christian faith says is that God will grant definitive justice to the victims of poverty and, by extension, to those who have sided with them. This is an active hope which unloosens creativity at all levels of human existence — intellectual, organizational, ecclesial — and which is marked by notable generosity and bound-less, even heroic altruism.

Such is the deepest reality of our world, and that is the

totality of its reality: it is a world of both sin and grace. The First World shows little or no interest in either aspect, but such is the reality from the perspective of the poor and the victimized.

In El Salvador we have also learned to ask ourselves what is truly human about human beings. To put it bluntly, we have learned to place under suspicion the Western understanding of the nature of humanity. There are many partially valid philosophical, theological and critical anthropologies. But historically and operatively these generally seem to suggest that what is human is "the way we are," or at least the way we imagine ourselves to be. Much political speechmaking and even much philosophical and theological discourse presuppose this notion, if in more subtle terms. The ideal which is consistently held up for all people is that of "modern man" or "Western man," even though here and there an occasional lament is voiced as to this ideal's failures and shortcomings.

The war in the Persian Gulf has shown, among other things, that the Western world has discovered or invented almost everything — except justice, solidarity and peace. The sum total of the West's scientific and technological knowledge, its impressive political democratic and Judeo-Christian traditions, the power it has amassed in its governments, its armies, its enterprises, its universities and its churches has not been sufficient to enable it to find a just and humane solution to conflict.

Yet despite this failure we continue to suppose that "we" know what it is to be human, and that everyone else must be like "us" in order to become human. The same dangerous premise holds sway in religious circles: primitively religious people must overcome any indigenous or superstitious elements in their Christianity before coming to be genuinely religious in today's world.

All of this has changed for me since returning to El Salvador. And the most important change is the very way of seeking the answer to the question of what it means to be human, coupled with the nagging suspicion that we have asked the question in a rather "dogmatic" and uncritical manner.

I am appalled at the triumphalist naïveté with which "human being" becomes interchangeable with "Western human being," when the truth of the matter is that the latter has not humanized anyone nor is himself or herself becoming more human. Those who lavish praise on Western individualism ignore how such an attitude has fostered insensibility toward the human community and even encouraged selfishness and aloofness. The Western capacity to achieve, to struggle and emerge victorious, has been so highly valued that it has enabled the Westerner to feel like a Prometheus, unneedful of anything or anyone else, including grace — a subject which, by the way, few First World philosophies and theologies know what to do with. Western human beings have to a great extent produced an inhuman world for those in the Third World and a dehumanizing world even in the First World. And still, no change seems imminent.

I am also appalled at the lack of a sense of history in Western efforts to understand humanity, as if there were a human essence which is replicated with slight variations throughout the planet. Of course, there is some truth to this view. But it is really an affront to continue to say to the many millions of the poor and the victimized that they are human beings "like everyone else," or to continue to exhort them to "hold out" because someday they will be like everyone else, complete with democracy and television sets.

In the face of this circumstance we need to place the human reality in historical context. We must realize that there are fundamental differences in the way people live. There are those who take life for granted and those who take anything but life for granted. To be a human being today has much to do, for instance, with whether one has food to eat.

At the level of human worth it might be said that things are improving, since the modern world, the U.S. Constitution, the United Nations' Declaration of Human Rights and so on have all proclaimed equal rights for all human beings. But that is not the way things are. Whether one has dignity, self-respect and rights depends to a great degree on an accident of birth; it helps considerably to have been born in the United States or Germany rather than in El Salvador or Pakistan.

Finally, I am troubled by the lack of dialectic in discussions about humanity. People naïvely speak of a common destiny for all humanity, ignoring the basic fact that a sharp division exists between those who have and those who do not — a gap which is ever growing.

We have discovered in El Salvador that we really did not know very precisely what it means to be a human being. Now, at least, I suspect that the mystery of the human being is not exhausted in what I knew before; there was much inhumanity in the ideal of humanity to which I formerly adhered. Above all, I have discovered that what is truly human has been showing itself to me where I once would have least expected it — in the faces of the poor. Although the mystery of what is human goes beyond any one particular instance, I have concluded that in order to comprehend our human essence, it is necessary to do so from the point of view not of the powerful but of the poor, and on their behalf. As the gospel says, the truth of the human being manifests itself in the Beatitudes of Jesus and in the parable of the good Samaritan.

From the perspective of the poor, we have rediscovered the need for a new kind of civilization, a civilization of poverty or at least of austerity, rather than one of impossible abundance for all — a civilization of work and not of capital, as Father Ellacuría would say. And that more humane civilization can be made concrete by considering first the community rather than the individual, by upholding transcendent values over crass pragmatism, by favoring celebration over mere diversion, and by emphasizing hope over calculated optimism and faith over positivism.

To come to know God, to hold and keep faith in God, is the ultimate mystery of the human being. It is not an easy thing to accomplish, and it cannot be achieved automatically from any perspective, not even a Salvadoran perspective. But I am convinced that true knowledge of God is facilitated in this milieu — at least of a God who resembles the God of Scripture — and faith in God becomes possible and sustainable here.

I believe in the God made manifest in Jesus, a God the Father who is a good God and on whom one can rely, a father who continues to be God and therefore will not let us be. To put it another way, I believe in the goodness and the mystery of God, and both of these have become sharply real to me in El Salvador.

The goodness of God is made real in the fact that God tenderly loves those dispossessed by life and identifies with the victims of this world. This fact can be difficult to accept in other places, but here it becomes patently clear and is reinforced in Scripture. A long-standing tradition has led us to think of a God who is directly universal, even though in reality this God is essentially a European and North American construct.

The mystery of God emerges even more clearly in this world of victims. For this is a God who not only favors the victimized but is at the mercy of their torturers. There are those who think that in a religious Latin America, faith in God is not as serious an issue as in the more secularized world. However, given the fact of so many victims, Latin America is the quintessential place to question God — as Job did, and as Jesus did from the cross — especially since God is confessed as a God of life. That God should permit victims to suffer and die is an insurmountable scandal. In the midst of such a situation, a believer can only accept the fact that God on the cross is as impotent as the victims themselves, and then interpret such impotency as God's way of being in solidarity with those victims. The cross on which God is placed is the most eloquent proclamation that God loves the victimized of this world. On that cross God's love is impotent yet believable. And it is from that perspective that the mystery of God must be reformulated.

Finally, from a Salvadoran perspective it is clear that the true God is at war with other gods. These are the idols, the false divinities — though they are real enough — which Archbishop Romero has concretized for our time in speaking of the absolutization of exploitive capitalism and "national security." Idols dehumanize their worshipers, but their ultimate evil lies in the fact that they demand victims in order to exist. If there is one single deep conviction which I have acquired in El Salvador, it is that such idols are real; they are not the inventions of so-called primitive peoples but are indeed active in modern societies. We dare not doubt this, in view of such idols' innumerable victims: the poor, the unemployed, the refugees, the detainees, the tortured, the disappeared, the massacred. And if idols do exist, then the issue of faith in God is very much alive.

I have also learned in El Salvador that to believe in God means to cease having faith in idols and to struggle against them. That is the reason why we humans must make a choice not only between faith and atheism but between faith and idolatry. In a world of victims, little can be known about a person simply because he calls himself a believer or a nonbeliever. It is imperative to know in which God she believes and against which idols she does battle. If such a person is truly a worshiper of idols, it matters little whether he accepts or denies the existence of a transcendent being. There really is nothing new in that: Jesus affirmed it in his parable of the last judgment.

So in order to speak the whole truth one must always say two things: in which God one believes and in which idol one does not believe. Without such a dialectic formulation, faith remains too abstract, is likely to be empty and, what is worse, can be very dangerous because it may very well allow for the coexistence of belief and idolatry.

Moreover, I have learned that to have faith in God means to do the will of God, to follow Jesus with the spirit of Jesus in the cause of God's kingdom. In El Salvador I have seen this faith quite clearly; innumerable martyrs have witnessed to it. I have learned that faith is difficult but entirely possible, that it is very costly but deeply humanizing. In El Salvador, God's solemn proclamation in the prophet Micah becomes very real: "What does the Lord require of you but to do justice, and to love kindness, and to walk humbly with your God?" To reproduce justice and love in human history is the way we respond to

God's love. To walk humbly throughout history is the way we respond to the mystery of God.

Such is the reality which has been revealing itself to us in El Salvador. In itself it is at once a clear clarion and good news. The reality which is a curse represents a call for us to transform it, but it also becomes a blessing and good news which transforms *us*. And these become one in the response of mercy toward crucified peoples.

In El Salvador we have rediscovered that the faithful response to this world of victims is the constant exercise of mercy, as in the parable of the good Samaritan, which Jesus uses to describe the true human being. The Samaritan sees someone wounded along the way, is moved to pity and cures his wounds. The importance of mercy in the gospels can be deduced also from the fact that Jesus himself and the Father who receives the prodigal son are described as being merciful.

We are speaking here not of "works of mercy" but rather of the basic structure of the response to this world's victims. This structure consists in making someone else's pain our very own and allowing that pain to move us to respond. We are to be moved simply by the fact that someone in need has been placed along our way. Even though Jesus presents the Samaritan as an example of one who obeys the commandment to love his neighbor, there is nothing in the parable which would lead us to conclude that the Samaritan acts in order to fulfill a commandment. He was simply moved to pity. It needs also to be emphasized that mercy is not only a fundamental attitude at the root of every human interaction but also a principle which affects subsequent interactions.

In El Salvador we have awakened to the fact that a heartless humanity manages to praise works of mercy but refuses to be guided by the mercy principle. Guided by this principle, we have discovered some important things.

First of all, we well know that in our world there are not just wounded individuals but crucified peoples, and that we should enflesh mercy accordingly. To react with mercy, then, means to do everything we possibly can to bring them down from the cross. This means working for justice, which is the name love acquires when it comes to entire majorities of people unjustly oppressed, and employing in behalf of justice all our intellectual, religious, scientific and technological energies.

Second, we must realize that mercy which becomes justice will automatically be persecuted by the powerful, and that therefore mercy must be clung to vigorously and consistently. The Salvadoran martyrs — alternately called subversives, communists and atheists — were merciful, consistently so. That is why they struggled for justice and that is why they were assassinated.

Third, we must give mercy priority above all else. This is no easy task for any civil institution, any government, business, political movement or army, nor for any religious or ecclesial institution. One must be willing to risk for mercy the way Archbishop Romero did, risking not only one's personal life but even the ecclesial institution itself. That is why he had to witness the destruction of his archdiocese's radio and printing operations, and why some of the priests around him were assassinated. All must be risked because what is first of all is the ultimate.

Fourth, I have learned that the exercise of mercy is the measure of freedom — that state of being universally hailed as a human ideal in the Western world. When he healed on a Sabbath, Jesus was violating the rules and norms of his time because he was merciful, not because he was a liberal. Jesus understood freedom from the point of view of mercy, not the other way around. For him freedom meant above all that nothing could stand in the way of the exercise of mercy.

This mercy is the demand which has been placed in our hearts by the Salvadoran reality. But the demand is also a blessing, is also good news. "Happy are the merciful," Jesus says. From this point we can reinterpret the other Beatitudes. "Happy are those who hunger and thirst for justice. Happy are those who work for peace. Happy are you when you are persecuted

for the cause of justice." And if we use the Beatitudes to reinterpret what we said above about acquiring new eyes, we can
also say, "Happy are those with a clean heart." Finally, if mercy
and new vision are placed at the service of the poor and we thus
participate to some degree in their lot, we too can hear, "Happy
are the poor."

The reader may be surprised that I have not mentioned
several topics which one might have expected to be discussed
in a piece coming from El Salvador. I have not spoken of liberation theology per se, nor of Marxism, nor of revolution, nor
of problems with the Vatican. True enough, the changes in Latin
America have brought about a new theology, a new way of being
church as a church of the poor, new relationships with popular
movements, new ways of solidarity and so on. But we have tried
to set forth what is at the root of these changes. Without the
roots, one cannot understand the changes.

To sum up, then: We have awakened from a sleep of inhumanity to a reality of humanity. We have learned to see God
from the point of view of the victimized, and we have tried to
see this world of the victimized from the point of view of God.
We have learned to exercise mercy and to find joy and a purpose
for life in doing so.

Remembering my dear Jesuit brother Ignacio Ellacuría,
rector of José Simeón Cañas Central American University, who
was murdered together with five other Jesuits and two pious
women on November 16, 1989, I have learned that there is
nothing as vital in order to live as a human being than to exercise
mercy on behalf of a crucified people, and that nothing is more
humanizing than to believe in the God of Jesus. As I have seen
this way of life become very real in many Salvadorans, in many
other Latin Americans and in many who sympathize with us in
various places, another new thing I have learned in El Salvador
is the importance of saying "Thank you," then life and faith still
make sense.

(Translated by Dimas Planas)

173

William C. Placher

Diversity, Community, Dialogue: How Their Minds Have Changed

The "How My Mind Has Changed" series is one of *The Christian Century*'s most venerable traditions, undertaken once a decade since 1939, when 34 contributors, Karl Barth and Reinhold Niebuhr among them, addressed the topic. By now each such collection represents a kind of milestone, an invitation to comparison and reflection on the state of the art of theology.

The current batch of essays reveals some intriguing and unexpected patterns. But it is important to stay modest and remember what they are patterns *in*. They do not survey the state of religion in 1990. To start with, all the authors are Christians, and even in America Christians increasingly recognize ourselves as only one element in a complex religious tapestry. All are white. All but Eberhard Jüngel and Jon Sobrino live in the U.S. They include sociologists and biblical scholars as well as theologians, but all except one (Richard John Neuhaus) teach

William C. Placher, who teaches at Wabash College in Crawfordsville, Indiana, recently wrote Unapologetic Theology: A Christian Voice in a Pluralistic Conversation *(Westminster/John Knox).*

in seminaries or universities. For the most part this is not only Christian theology and U.S. theology but *academic* theology — and therefore not, for instance, Jerry Falwell or M. Scott Peck or Shirley MacLaine or John Updike, to mention a widely diverse quartet whose members may have more influence on the religious lives of more North Americans than those included here.

I confess that the words from beyond our borders — those of Jüngel and Sobrino — spoke to me most powerfully of all, but theirs are in some ways the least typical essays. My task is summary and generalization, and this particular collection primarily reflects some concerns common among U.S. theologians. Whether one approves or disapproves of them, the patterns are worth examining.

The points of view gathered here represent a cross-section of thoughtful participant-observers in the business of thinking seriously about Christian faith. They include a range of very different voices, from committed liberationists to angry neo-conservatives, with revisionists, postliberals and an evangelical scattered in between. It is probably significant that four of the 14 are women; two women were included a decade ago, and never more than one before that. It is also worth remembering, in fairness to the editors, that some of those asked to write declined or failed to come through on schedule. Journalism is an imperfect social science.

The essays defy quick summary. At least in retrospect (did it seem so at the time?) the neo-orthodox giants, Barth and Niebuhr, dominate that first collection 50 years ago. Ten years ago it was liberation theologians who spoke with most powerful conviction. No single perspective stands out in these essays. Indeed, the best way I could find to summarize the collection was to imagine a dialogue in which a number of quite distinct voices get to speak for themselves; you can judge my success at the end of this essay.

In the midst of such pluralism, it might seem paradoxical that the most common theme is *community*. That emphasis on community takes varied forms and has inspirations as diverse as Latin American base communities, feminist collectives, and Alasdair MacIntyre's vision of a new St. Benedict who will help us find the communal virtues to rescue us from the chaos of a new Dark Ages. But whatever inspires it, community keeps popping up as theme. Stanley Hauerwas celebrates the virtues of friendship and concrete community and calls for a theology in service to the community of the church. Robert Bellah laments the "religious individualism" of some of his earlier works; he *has* changed his mind. Thomas Oden rejoices in his own immersion in the community of traditional exegesis reaching back to the patristic era. Sallie McFague calls for more collegiality in theological work — both in the simple sense of dividing up the labor and in the more complex nurturing of the virtues that make such cooperative work possible. Eberhard Jüngel talks about how encountering the church as a place of truth and freedom in the midst of East Germany made him a theologian. Jon Sobrino points out the dangers of Western individualism. Carter Heyward attacks the selfishness of the age of Reagan and expresses gratitude for the ways in which — having long talked about community — she has found particular communities to help her through problems in her own life. The list could continue. Even Peter Berger's frustration that he cannot locate a theologically liberal Protestant church that has not fallen victim to "left-liberal-liberationist politics" and therefore finds himself "ecclesiastically homeless" betrays a yearning for community, valued in its absence.

It would badly distort the diversity of these essays to conclude that all these references to community represent different versions of the same story. As Hauerwas keeps reminding us, communities tell stories and inculcate virtues, but different communities tell different stories and foster different virtues. If many of these folk celebrate or long for community, one cannot imagine the community that would occasion all their celebrations or satisfy all their longings.

Preoccupation with community always risks looking inward too much. (Any position entails risks; its proponents need not fall victim to them.) The first essay in the 1970 series was Robert McAfee Brown's, and the cover of that issue showed him against the background of the White House, reading a statement about Vietnam. The picture captured the mood of the time, reflected in many of the essays. This time around, by my count only three of the U.S. contributors mention any political, economic or military event of the 1980s (and Sallie McFague's eloquent discussion of the ecological crisis is the only article from the U.S. to address such issues at length). The silence is more dramatic given the contrast with Jüngel's powerful reflections on the revolutions of Eastern Europe and Sobrino's eloquent remembrance of the martyrs of El Salvador. It is even odder given that considerably more authors mention political events of the 1960s.

I came of age in the '60s myself, and like many of my generation am always willing to believe that, compared to the excitements of our youth, the '80s have been a pretty dull time. But consider: Eastern Europe and the Middle East, continuing crisis in Latin America, the U.S. shift from being the world's banker to being its biggest debtor, an AIDS epidemic, a crack epidemic, further steps toward various ecological catastrophes, maybe the beginnings of real change in South Africa, Reagan, Gorbachev. Whatever their faults, the '80s were hardly dull. So it says something about the focus of much recent theological thinking in the U.S. that such events get mentioned so rarely.

A second point may be related. The series' title invites reflection about change, allowing for "staying the same" only parenthetically and grudgingly. Ten years ago, most essayists had no trouble with that assignment. They talked about intellectual "peregrinations" (Peter Berger), "being theologically still in passage" (Langdon Gilkey), a "stimulating and challenging" decade that had expanded one's horizons (John Hick), "movement in a great variety of directions" (Rosemary Radford Ruether), and so on. James Gustafson even declared himself uncomfortable with "How My Mind Has Changed" because it implied that he had at some point made up his mind and stopped moving, only to start up again subsequently. Why not, he asked, call the series "How My Thinking Has Been Developing"? Back in 1939, for that matter, Reinhold Niebuhr started things off with characteristic vigor: "About midway in my ministry . . . I underwent a fairly complete conversion of thought which involved rejection of almost all the liberal theological ideals and ideas with which I ventured forth in 1915."

This time around, two writers (Oden and Elizabeth Achtemeier) pointedly begin by saying that they find their minds essentially *un*changed. Several cautiously say that others could probably tell how they have changed better than they can themselves — one implication being, surely, that the changes are not all that obvious. Others talk far more about changes around them (often regretted) than changes in themselves. They may have deepened or grown, but, if these authors have *moved,* they rarely choose to talk about it. It is often the pressure of external events that produces dramatic change. The silence about movement may be related to the silence about politics.

As already noted, all but one of these authors live in the U.S. What is striking is the U.S.-centeredness of their essays. In earlier decades, many theologians in this country deferred to "theological giants" who, almost by definition, lived somewhere else. Ten years ago, many theologians here were emphasizing how much we in privileged lands need to learn from voices of the Third World. This time around, the contributors most often mentioned books and authors from our own country.

Is that a good thing? No, and yes. On the negative side, our world is not growing less interdependent. Christianity is growing most in the southern hemisphere, and its most dramatic experiences as this decade was ending were in the eastern hemisphere. So should we not be paying more attention? "The First World," Sobrino says, "is not interested in the Third World."

On the other hand, self-sufficiency can be a sign of maturity. We no longer need to think of "real scholars" as a breed living elsewhere. If we want to listen to voices long repressed, it may sometimes be most important (and most painful) to listen to those closest to hand. The theme of community recurs: looking first close to hand can be a cop-out, but it can also be the honest starting point for practical action.

A parallel point: ten years ago interreligious dialogue provided the central theme for a number of articles. This time, connections with non-Christian religions figure less prominently; it is the life of Christian churches that gets more attention. Again, a matter of looking close to home — maybe narrow, maybe more practically honest.

If the geographical center of these essays lies in the U.S., the ecclesiastical center seems to be in Roman Catholicism. Neuhaus has been arguing that we live in the midst of "the Catholic moment," and this collection bears him out. Catholic writers discuss developments in their own church; Protestants like Oden, Lindbeck, Hauerwas and Neuhaus (who announced his conversion to Roman Catholicism after he wrote his article) talk about the ways Catholic thought has influenced them. Berger says he would find it almost impossible to "move toward Rome," but the idea has apparently crossed his mind.

No doubt the grass always seems greener on the other side of the fence, and in some moods Catholic theologians these days must envy Protestants our greater freedoms. But Protestants, I suspect, often see Catholicism as a place where major theologians help shape official church documents, seminary education is still deeply theological, and what theologians write still matters. It might be nice to seem important enough to be dangerous.

That may be a thought to comfort feminists as they read these essays. Ten years ago Letty Russell and Rosemary Radford Ruether defended feminism; the male contributors sympathized or ignored them, but no one directly attacked them. Carl Henry warned against the dangers from the left in the churches' flirtations with socialism and religious pluralism, but he did not mention women's issues. Berger was writing then

179

about what he had learned from the Third World. This time Berger, Neuhaus, Achtemeier and Oden all see feminism in one form or another as a central danger to the life of the church. Even Elisabeth Schüssler Fiorenza, while remaining an untamed feminist, warns against some tendencies in the movement.

Having irate enemies is no doubt one of the prices of success. One can be certain that 50 years ago, or even ten, not everyone writing for *The Christian Century* was convinced of the truth of feminism; for many, its issues would not even have seemed worth debating. Many women and men concerned about these issues will find the triumphant feminism described in a couple of these essays hard to reconcile with the world or the churches they experience, where women still struggle for equality in all kinds of ways, but the conviction of some that we have gone too far is perhaps a warning to reconsider *some* changes and at least a sure sign that we *have* been in motion.

These essays thus reflect a political debate with important implications for the future of the churches — call it a debate between liberationists and neoconservatives. That debate reaches beyond feminism to a host of social issues that divide many denominations — with the kind of people who read, and write for, the *Century* sometimes on both sides of the debate.

Another debate also kept emerging in this collection — a dispute about theological method. In his essay for this series ten years ago, David Tracy gave one of the best short accounts of his "revisionist theology." It is theology in the tradition of Paul Tillich, anxious to reach out to political allies and intellectual points of contact in the wider culture, and Tracy remains its most thoughtful defender.

One significant theological event of the past decade was the publication of George Lindbeck's *Nature of Doctrine* in 1983. Lindbeck set out a different way of thinking about theology — he called it "postliberal theology" — with theological roots more in Karl Barth and Lindbeck's colleague Hans Frei than in Tillich, but with other antecedents in Wittgenstein and anthropologists and literary critics. Postliberal theology emphasizes the need to clarify the distinctively Christian point of view, to tell the stories that shape the distinctive language of the Christian community. Given the importance of community throughout these essays, it is not surprising that one sees elements of "postliberalism" not only in Lindbeck and Hauerwas but also in Neuhaus, Bellah and others.

Still, postliberal theology too remains one view among others, certainly not a dominant perspective. In the theological world which these essays capture, no one point of view carries the day. As I noted earlier, as I struggled to think how to summarize these essays, I found myself imagining a debate among different voices. Perhaps a revisionist and a postliberal had just been arguing . . .

LIBERATIONIST: In a world where people are suffering as the victims of oppression, your debates about theological method often seem to me academic in the worst sense of the word, irrelevant to real people's real problems.

REVISIONIST: No doubt we often get too lost in technical issues, but I hope my theology really does matter to people's lives.

POSTLIBERAL: And I'd say the same.

LIBERATIONIST: But how?

POSTLIBERAL: Christians believe in a God who cares about the oppressed. But our society has often — perhaps especially in the 1980s — proclaimed a very different set of values — the values of brutal competition for material success and military power. At least for a while, this was the decade of "greed is good," and the new decade now begins with unbridled confidence in the effectiveness of military force. So Christians have to speak up in their own distinctive voice and pose a radical challenge to those values. We have to say, as clearly as we can, that we stand for something different.

REVISIONIST: I don't believe in those materialistic values either. But if we Christians are going to make a difference in society, we can't retreat to a little ghetto and just "be the church" in the way that Stanley Hauerwas or even George Lindbeck sometimes call us to do. We have to be open to hearing other voices. We have to admit that Christians have sometimes been part of the forces that oppressed. We have to make connections and alliances with non-Christians. And that means we can't simply repeat the Christian story as if in a vacuum.

NEOCONSERVATIVE: I have the suspicion that by "materialistic values" you really mean capitalism. If the '80s have taught us anything, it is that Marxism doesn't work. It's only intellectuals and church bureaucrats infatuated with liberation theology who keep up this romantic attack on capitalistic values.

LIBERATIONIST: Waving the red flag once again! Liberation theology can't be equated with Marxism and never could be. Feminists and African-Americans interested in liberation thought have rarely accepted a Marxist agenda, and even Latin American liberation theologians almost always made their differences with doctrinaire Marxists quite clear.

NEOCONSERVATIVE: And yet I still hear the Marxist rhetoric.

LIBERATIONIST: Sure, like most social theorists these days, including many of those you neoconservatives admire, we've learned some things from Marx. We recognize that "sin" manifests itself in the things people do as part of institutions and groups as well as in what they do as individuals, and that changing people often involves changing their social context. That doesn't make us Stalinists. If you've noticed, many of the Eastern Europeans whose revolutions you profess to admire have some real criticisms about the values of Western capitalism too.

NEOCONSERVATIVE: I doubt that we're going to agree on these issues. In the meantime, we've interrupted a discussion between our two friends here about theological method, a discussion I was finding interesting. I confess I find myself sympathetic to what I understand of this "postliberal theology." It seems to be saying that the church should stop signing up with political causes and get on with the business of being the church.

182

POSTLIBERAL: I'm not sure I really want you as an ally. Yes, I think we ought to recover a biblical view of things, but I also think that biblical view turns out to be pretty radical in a number of respects. I agree that we can't latch on to the fads of contemporary culture — but I suspect you want to latch on to economic conservativism and American nationalism.

LIBERATIONIST: In some respects, I can see that the biblical view is pretty radical. But in others it isn't. It condemns homosexuality. It takes slavery for granted. It supports the values of a patriarchal society. So this vision of "letting the biblical world absorb our world" — how can I be comfortable with that?

REVISIONIST: It's not only politically wrong; it's methodologically naïve. So many contemporary literary critics and historians and philosophers remind us that we can't just pick up a story and read it as it is — we always bring assumptions and values and questions. We ought to be honest about that, rather than pretending to engage in a sort of naïve reading. And that honesty requires that we think about some issues in contemporary philosophy relevant to what we're doing.

POSTLIBERAL: That sounds to me like letting some philosophical system shape the way we understand the gospel.

REVISIONIST: That's not what I said. I said that aspects of our contemporary experience will inevitably shape our reading in some ways, and it's healthier and more honest to admit the fact and try to analyze it.

LIBERATIONIST: But you're getting off the subject. What worries me is that we can't just buy the biblical view of things without buying into a lot of oppression.

POSTLIBERAL: But once you start using the values of our culture to judge the biblical message, then neoconservatism stands a good chance of carrying the day — it surely does represent a great many of the values of our culture.

NEOCONSERVATIVE: And proud of it, too. The rest of you seem to be so removed from what's really going on in the churches. I find all sorts of people like me who wish we could worship

God rather than having a political agenda crammed down our throats. Until the "mainstream" churches get that message, they're just going to keep shrinking in size.

POSTLIBERAL: A smaller, more committed church that knew what it believed might be a more faithful church.

REVISIONIST: I'm not sure we need to shrink into irrelevance — not if we find ways to make alliances with a range of people throughout our culture . . .

I didn't hear the end of that conversation. On the evidence of these essays, it has not ended but still vigorously continues, with other voices joining in. If such discussions have not yet produced answers, they are surely asking some of the right questions: how to do theology, how to connect it with our lives and our world. Tune in again in ten years. Better yet, stay tuned in the meantime.